baby knits for beginners

baby knits for beginners

Debbie Bliss

EBURY PRESS
LONDON

First published in Great Britain in 2003

3 5 7 9 10 8 6 4

Text © Debbie Bliss 2003
Photographs © Sandra Lousada 2003

First published by Ebury Press
Random House, 20 Vauxhall Bridge Road,
London SW1V 2SA

Random House Australia (Pty) Limited
20 Alfred Street, Milsons Point, Sydney,
New South Wales 2061, Australia

Random House New Zealand Limited
18 Poland Road, Glenfield, Auckland 10, New Zealand

Random House South Africa (Pty) Limited
Endulini, 5A Jubilee Road, Parktown 2193, South Africa

The Random House Group Limited Reg. No. 954009

www.randomhouse.co.uk

A CIP catalogue record for this book is available from the British Library.

Editor: Emma Callery
Designer: Christine Wood
Photographer: Sandra Lousada
Stylist: Sammie Bell
Pattern checker: Rosy Tucker

ISBN 0 09 188913 8

Papers used by Ebury Press are natural, recyclable products made from wood grown in sustainable forests.

Printed and bound in Singapore by Tien Wah Press

contents

introduction

Many first-time knitters are attracted to the craft when they are looking for something special to make for a new baby. Surrounded as we are by mass-produced garments, creating a hand knit gives us the opportunity to invest into every stitch the love and care we feel for our own baby or one of a friend or family. Everything we knit is unique, however many other people have made the same pattern; every knit or purl we work reflects our individuality. Small garments also give the new knitter the opportunity to experience the excitement and satisfaction of completing a project more quickly than when tackling one for an adult. When learning anything new it is important to feel that the finished design is always in sight, especially when you are perhaps struggling for a time with a new technique.

Each project here features a new technique or a new stage in developing your understanding of the craft, from the simple garter stitch scarf to the final design, a V-neck sweater with pockets and fully fashioned shapings. There are clear, easy-to-follow diagrams at the beginning of the book, which are then repeated when a particular technique is used in a pattern. The techniques have been repeated both to help the reader and to emphasise the stage that she/he has reached. As well as concentrating on the basics, I have also explained pattern instructions that I have found even experienced knitters sometimes find confusing – things such as turning rows or creating square set-in sleeves.

Although most of the designs are very simple, I have designed them to be attractive and stylish in their own right rather than just exercises in technique. I have kept the styles classic as one of the joys of knitting for babies is that if the garments are well looked after they can be handed on to others and down to future generations. I have also used my own yarn ranges, which I feel are perfect for knitting for babies, with soft cottons, cashmere mixes and merino wool to wrap around or snuggle into. Child friendly, they are easy to wash and wear.

knitting essentials

yarns

Your knitting essentials will always begin with your yarn and needles. We are lucky to be around at a time when there is so much choice to be had in the variety of wonderful yarns that are available and a selection of needles to suit all types of knitting and preferences. Here is a guide to yarns in general and to the ones used in this book.

yarn fibres

Fibres are divided into two main categories, natural and synthetic. Natural fibres are then divided into animal fibres, such as wool, angora, cashmere and silk, and those from vegetable fibres, such as cotton, linen and hemp. Synthetic fibres are made from polyester, nylon and acrylic. Synthetic fibres tend to get a bad press and for good reason. Although they are cheaper and can be thrown into a washing machine, they don't have the same insulating properties and can a produce limp, flat fabric, which will melt on contact with an iron. However, blended with natural yarns they can add durability and lightness.

yarn plies

Yarn is also made up from one or more strands of yarn called plies. Plied yarn comes from several plies of yarn twisted together. The thickness of a yarn comes not from the number of plies but the individual thickness of each ply. For instance, a 4-ply yarn can be finer than a single-ply heavy yarn. Yarns with a tight twist are usually strong and smooth and those with a looser twist are generally softer and less even. They can pull apart if over-handled and may not be suitable for sewing up your garment.

yarn weights

Yarns come in different weights or thicknesses and range from fine 2- or 3-ply yarns to bulky, chunky yarns. The thickness of the yarn determines how many stitches and rows there are to 2.5cm (1in) and is the basis on which all knitting patterns are created.

the most commonly used yarns

4-ply: a fine yarn knitted on 3¼mm (US 3) needles. The tension is usually 28 sts to 10cm (4in).
Lightweight yarn: this is a yarn that is slightly thicker than a 4-ply and is worked on the same-sized needles. It is between a 4-ply and a double knitting yarn. The tension is usually 25 sts to 10cm (4in).
Double knitting: often referred to as DK, this yarn is knitted on 4mm (US 6) needles. The tension is usually 22 sts to 10cm (4in).

Aran weight: slightly thicker than a DK and traditionally used in Aran or fisherman sweaters, aran is knitted on 4½mm (US 7) or 5mm (US 8) needles. The tension is usually 18 sts to 10cm (4in).
Chunky: knitted on 6½mm (US 10) needles, the tension is usually 14 sts to 10cm (4in).

You may come across these yarn terms when choosing yarn.

Wool: wool spun from the fleece of sheep is the yarn that is the most commonly associated with knitting. It has many great qualities as it is durable, elastic and warm in the winter. Merino wool is from the oldest breed of sheep and is considered the finest wool yarn. Lamb's wool comes from a lamb's first shearing and pure new wool is used to describe wool that is made straight from the fleece and is not recycled.
Cotton: cotton is made from a natural plant fibre. It is an ideal all-seasons yarn as it is warm in the winter and cool in the summer. It also shows up stitch detail well, which makes it ideal when you have subtle stitch patterns such as moss stitch, particularly where it is used as detailing. Generally it does not have the elasticity of wool.
Cotton and wool: using a yarn that is a combination of cotton and wool is particularly good for children's wear because the wool fibres give it elasticity while the cotton content is perfect for children who find wool irritating against the skin.
Cashmere: cashmere is made from the under hair of a particular Asian goat. It is associated with the ultimate in luxury and is unbelievably soft to the touch. If combined with merino and microfibre, as in my cashmerino range, it is a perfect yarn for babies.
Smooth yarns: these tend to be the yarns with the tighter twist. They are sometimes also referred to as classic yarns. The smooth surface makes them perfect for showing up stitches, which is particularly important with subtle stitch patterns or cables.
Fancy or novelty yarns: these yarns tend to be part of a fashion trend for a particular season. They are often textured, such as the curly looking bouclé, or may be a shiny ribbon yarn. They do not always have a very long shelf life so knit it while you can, or if it is for a project that you are going to put on the back burner, make sure you have enough yarn!
Blends: yarns made from a mix of fibres, such as wool/cotton, cotton/silk. They can often combine the best of both worlds, for instance the elasticity of wool with the coolness of cotton.
Marls: yarns of two or more plies where the plies are different colours.
Tweeds: yarns with a background shade contrasting with flecks of different colours.
Random or variegated yarns: these have been dyed with different shades along the length of the yarn. They can be a good way of achieving colour effects without having to change yarn and colours.

Felted yarns: these have been treated so that when knitted they give the soft and fuzzy appearance of felted fabric.

Heathers: yarns that combine grey fleece yarn with dyed yarns giving a soft, muted look.

Debbie Bliss yarns

The following are descriptions of my yarns and a guide to their weights and types. All the yarns used in the book are machine washable.

Debbie Bliss merino aran: a 100% merino wool in an aran or fisherman weight. Approximately 78m/50g ball.

Debbie Bliss wool/cotton: a 50% merino wool, 50% cotton lightweight yarn blend that is between a 4-ply and a double knitting weight. Approximately 107m/50g ball.

Debbie Bliss cotton double knitting: a 100% cotton in a double knitting weight. Approximately 84m/50g ball.

Debbie Bliss cashmerino aran: a 55% merino wool, 33% microfibre, 12% cashmere yarn in an aran or fisherman weight. Approximately 90m/50g ball.

Debbie Bliss baby cashmerino: a 55% merino wool, 33% microfibre, 12% cashmere lightweight yarn between a 4-ply and a double knitting weight. Approximately 125m/50g ball.

buying yarn

Always try to buy the yarn specified in the pattern. The designer will have created the design with that yarn in mind and a substitute may produce a garment that is different from the one that you had wanted to make. For instance, the design may rely for its appeal on a subtle stitch pattern, which is lost when using a yarn of inferior quality. Or by replacing a natural yarn such as cotton with a synthetic fibre you may end up with a limp fabric and the freshness and crispness of the original fabric lost. No manufacturer will accept responsibility for problems you may have with the sizing of a pattern if a different yarn has been used.

If you do decide to substitute a yarn, buy one that is the same weight and, where possible, the same fibre content. It is essential to use a yarn that has the same tension or your measurements will be different from the original design. The garment will have been designed to specific proportions and a difference in tension may mean the boxy sweater you fell in love with has become a skinny tunic.

You will also need to check meterage or yardage. The fibre content and make up of the yarn determine how much yarn you get for the weight. In other words, two 50g balls may have different lengths of yarn, so you may need to buy more or less yarn than that quoted in the pattern.

By checking the ball band on the yarn you will have nearly all the information you need before you start your project.

the ball band

Yarn weight: the company's name and brand name will tell you whether you have the right yarn for the design. There may be different weights of yarn within the same named range so make sure you haven't picked up, for instance, the double knitting quality of the range when you needed the aran weight. The tension and needles quoted on the band will also help you here. A standard double knitting weight is usually 22 sts to 10cm (4in) and knitted on 4mm (US 6) needles. An aran weight is usually 18 sts and knitted on 4½mm (US 7) needles.

The metreage or yardage: the length will inform you as to whether you need to buy fewer or more balls if you are substituting a yarn. The weight will tell you in grams or ounces the weight of the ball. This is also important to check if you are not using the yarn quoted. It is all too easy to buy eight 50g balls and then on rereading the pattern realise the original yarn was in 100g balls and you should have bought double the amount.

Fibre content: this will tell you, for example, whether the yarn is cotton, wool, acrylic or a blend, and care instructions will let you know whether the finished garment should be hand-washed, machine-washed or dry-cleaned.

Dye lot number: check this because yarns are dyed in batches or lots, which can sometimes vary considerably. Your retailer may not have the same dye lot later so try to buy all your yarn for your project at the same time. If you know that sometimes you use more yarn than that quoted in the pattern, buy more yarn initially. If it is not possible to buy all the yarn you need with the same dye lot, work the borders such as cuffs, ribs or collar in the odd one as it is less likely to show.

equipment

When you are ready to learn to knit you will need, first and foremost, yarn, knitting needles and scissors.

knitting needles

Knitting needles come in a variety of materials, sizes, styles and prices. As you progress you will begin to use the type of needles that suit you best.

Knitting needles have been around for a very long time and have been made in a variety of materials from ivory to whalebone. Since they were first mass produced in steel they have been made in wood, aluminium, plastic and more. For beginners I would recommend bamboo needles as they have a silky finish, which lets the stitches glide across the needle and are good for clammy hands, one of the disadvantages of the new, nervous knitter!

There are three types of needle: straight, circular and double pointed. Straight knitting needles are sold in pairs and come in three lengths. You will need longer needles for work that is wider or if you need to pick up a lot of stitches – for instance, down the front edges of a jacket. A pattern should tell you if you need to use longer needles. Circular and double pointed needles are usually used for circular knitting when there is no seam.

A needle's size is determined by its diameter; the smaller the needle, the smaller the size of the stitch, and vice versa. Finer yarns are worked on smaller needles and bulkier yarns on larger ones. If you are not able to achieve the tension or number of stitches and rows to 2.5cm (1 in) that the pattern states then you will need to change your needle size to obtain the size of stitch required (see Tension on page 34). Needle sizes range from 2mm (US 0) to 9mm (US 15).

scissors

Scissors are important as they save you from the temptation of breaking off yarn with your teeth! A pair of small scissors with sharp points is the best, preferably with a case if you are going to be carrying them around with your knitting.

tape measure and darning needle

As you progress from practice squares you will also need a tape measure marked with centimetres and inches to measure your tension square and a blunt darning or tapestry needle to sew up seams.

non-essential but helpful tools

● A row counter that you can put on the end of your needle so you can check row numbers.
● A stitch holder to secure stitches, such as at a front neck that you are going to work later.
● Safety pins to use as mini stitch holders or to mark where you have made increases on a sleeve, for example.

buttons

Buttons chosen in a hurry or without much thought can really spoil a garment while the right ones add charm and style. There is a huge variety to choose from but if your local store doesn't have any that inspire you, try charity shops to see if you can find vintage ones. You are more likely to find ones you like in a small, rather old-fashioned yarn shop where they may be carrying old stock than in a modern department store.

Children often like to choose their own buttons with nursery images such as ducks or teddies, and pewter or metallic buttons can look great on denim-style yarns. If I am unsure of the type or colour of button that would suit my design, I often choose mother-of-pearl, which not only give a look of quality to a garment but also pick up and reflect the shade of the yarn.

Make sure you sew buttons on a garment for a baby really securely – small children love to fiddle with them or suck them.

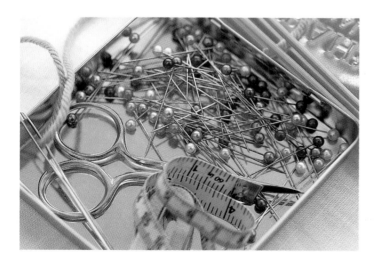
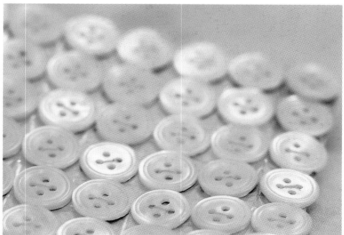

reading pattern instructions

I used to tell readers to read the pattern carefully before starting but I have changed my views on this as I feel that some parts of the pattern, which are simple and make sense when you are actually knitting them, seem confusing when initially reading through them. Some instructions may only really make sense when the knitting is on the needles.

However, do read the materials list before you leave the shop with your pattern and yarn. Check the equipment you need carefully. There is nothing worse than getting home, eager to start your project, only to find out that you don't have the needle size you need. Check too for additional materials that you may need, such as a zip or buttons. However, buttons should sometimes be left until the garment is completed to get a proper idea of size or shade.

check measurements

Look at the measurements on the knitting instructions before buying your yarn to be sure what size you want to knit. Most patterns quote the actual finished knitted size of the garment rather than the bust/chest measurements of the wearer. The actual measurements will show the width around the whole garment and this will tell you how much 'ease' a garment has, whether it is a generous style or slim fitting. If you wish to make up a garment with a different fit from that in the pattern, you may decide to knit a smaller or larger size. If you are unsure, measure an existing garment for comparison. The length of the garment is usually taken from the cast-on edge to the shoulder.

look through the abbreviations

There is rarely space in a knitting pattern to write out all the instructions in full. For this reason abbreviations are sometimes used throughout the pattern. They are explained in full before the start of the pattern or, if in a book, on a page dedicated to abbreviations. As you gain in experience you will become familiar with the most common ones such as 'k' for knit and 'beg' for beginning. Not all abbreviations mean the same in different patterns so check them carefully. There are also some phrases that appear in patterns that you may need to get familiar with.

abbreviations

alt = alternate
beg = beginning
cm = centimetre(s)
cont = continue
dec = decrease
foll = following
in = inch(es)
inc = increase one st by working into front and back of st
K(k) = knit
kfb = knit into front and back of st
m1 = make one st
mm = millimetres
patt = pattern
P(p) = purl
rem = remaining
rep = repeat
st(s) = stitch(es)
skpo = slip 1, k1, pass slipped st over
sl = slip
st st = stocking stitch
tbl = through back loop
tog = together
yf = yarn forward
yon = yarn over needle
yrn = yarn round needle

most frequently used phrases

RS/Right side: refers to the right side of the fabric – the side that is facing to the outside when the garment is worn.
WS/Wrong side: refers to the wrong side of the fabric – the side that is facing to the inside when worn.
At the same time: two things need to done at the same time, for instance decreasing on a neckline at the same time as an armhole is being shaped.

Work as for: you will be working the piece as a previous one, as in 'work as for back'.

Ending with a RS row: the last row you work will be a right side row.

Ending with a WS row: the last row you work will be a wrong side row.

Inc every 4th row: work 3 rows straight and then increase on the next row. This is the same principle for other increasings, as in every 5th row. This is commonly found on sleeves.

Work inc sts into pattern: this is usually found on a sleeve where you are increasing stitches. You need to make sure you keep the repeat of the stitch pattern consistent on each side of the sleeve as you add on more stitches.

other points to remember

● When working a jacket or cardigan where you have two front pieces, remember that the Right Front refers to the right front as you are wearing it rather than as you are looking at it.

● Most patterns are written for a range of sizes. Quantities and measurements relating to the smallest size are given first in the instructions and appear outside of the round ( ) brackets. Those for the larger sizes are given inside the brackets. Make sure as you follow the pattern that you are consistently using the right stitches for your size – it is only too easy to switch sizes inside the brackets. One way to avoid this is to photocopy the pattern and then mark the size you are knitting with a highlighter pen.

● Work the instructions given in square [ ] brackets the number of times stated afterwards, as in [k1, p1] 3 times. Where 0 appears, no stitches or rows are worked for this size.

● Asterisks are also used to indicate a repeat, as in * k1, p1, rep from * twice.

When two parts of a garment share the same instructions, asterisks are also used, as in rep from * to **. This means repeat the instructions between the asterisks.

care of garments

Taking care of your garments is important. If you have invested all that time and labour in knitting them, you want them to look good for as long as possible. Follow these guidelines for the best results.

1 Check the yarn label for washing instructions. Most yarns can now be machine-washed on a delicate wool cycle (all the yarns used in this book are machine-washable).
2 Prior to washing make a note of the measurements of the garment or piece, such as the width and length.
3 After washing, lay the garment flat and check the measurements again to see if they are the same. If not, smooth and pat back into shape.

Some knitters still prefer to hand wash their garments. Use soap flakes especially created for hand knits, and warm rather than hot water. Handle the knits gently in the water – do not rub or wring as this can stretch or felt the fabric. Rinse well to get rid of any soap and squeeze out excess water. Even if you have machine-washed your garment, the gentle spin will mean that you will probably need to get rid of more water by rolling the garment in a towel. Dry the garment by laying it out flat on top of a towel to absorb moisture, smooth and pat into shape. Do not dry knits next to direct heat such as a radiator. Store them loosely folded to allow the air to circulate.

Debbie Bliss
wool/cotton

beginning to knit

casting on

The first step when beginning to knit is to cast on. There are several ways of doing this, but there are two cast ons – the thumb and the cable methods – that seem to be the most frequently used. The best one to choose is the one that you feel most comfortable with, or that produces the kind of edge you prefer. You may choose to use a different cast-on technique depending on where it occurs on the garment. The cable cast on, for example, produces a firm edge that can be useful in an area that may get a lot of wear, such as on sleeve cuffs.

holding needles

Some knitters hold their right needle like a pen, some like a knife. I prefer to knit in the 'pen' style as I find it helps me knit more quickly and more fluently. Try this first, as illustrated below, and then try holding it over the needle and see which you feel more comfortable with.

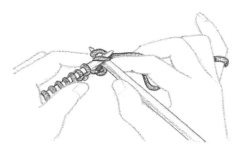

To hold the yarn in your right hand, pass it around your little finger, under your centre finger and over your index finger. Your index finger is used to pass the yarn around the tip of the needle. The yarn circled around your little finger creates the necessary tension for even knitting.

starting with a slip knot

To start most cast-on methods, you first need to make a simple slip knot, also called a 'slip loop'. This makes the slip knot the very first 'stitch' that you cast onto your knitting needle. To make it clear which end of the yarn comes from the yarn ball, the loose end is shown short so it fits in the diagram – but in reality you should leave a long loose end so it can either be darned in or used to sew the seam.

1 Wind the yarn twice around fingers on your left hand to make a circle of yarn as shown in the inset. With the knitting needle, pull a loop of the yarn attached to the ball through the yarn circle on your fingers.

2 Then pull both ends of the yarn to tighten the slip knot on the knitting needle. You are now ready to use one of the following cast-on methods to cast stitches onto your knitting needle.

thumb cast on (English)

I use the thumb cast on because, as a fairly tight knitter, I find it gives me a fast, fluid cast on with an edge that I like. It has quite a bit of 'give' in it, which makes it ideal for edges that need some flexibility and stretch, for instance on the roll-up brim of a beanie hat (see Simple hat on page 72).

One word of warning, however – because you are casting on and working towards the end of the yarn (unlike two-needle methods where you work towards the ball), you have to predict how much yarn is needed for the amount of stitches required. You may find that you are left with a few more stitches to make and not enough yarn to make them with. Depending on the thickness of the yarn, 1m (39in) creates about 100 stitches.

1 Make a slip knot as shown previously, leaving a long tail. With the slip knot on the needle in your right hand and the yarn that comes from the ball over your index finger, wrap the tail end of the yarn over your left thumb from front to back. Secure the yarn in your left palm with your fingers.

2 Then insert the knitting needle upwards through the yarn loop on your left thumb.

However, if you are unsure, over-compensate by allowing more yarn than you think you need. You can always use the extra length to sew up the seams.

Generally, knitters are taught to use a slip knot to begin with when casting on with this method, but once you become confident with the technique, rather than use a slip knot, work the first stitch by simply laying the yarn over your thumb from front to back and holding the yarn as before with the yarn over the right needle – then knit into the thumb loop. I find that this gives a slightly neater edge to the cast on. These diagrams have been drawn with the hand holding the needles like a knife, over the needles (see Holding needles, page 24).

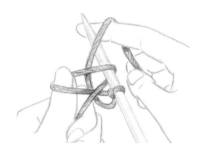

3 Next, with the right index finger, wrap the yarn from the ball up and over the point of the knitting needle.

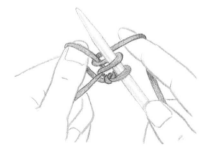

4 Then draw the yarn through the loop on your thumb to form a new stitch on the knitting needle. Lastly, let the yarn loop slip off your left thumb and pull the loose end to tighten up the stitch. Repeat these steps to make the stitches you need.

cast-on tip
On reversible fabrics, after casting on you can decide which is the wrong side of the fabric. You can then check this by noticing whether the 'tail' of your cast-on yarn is on the left- or right-hand side of the work. With the thumb cast on, this tail will be at the opposite end of the work to the cable cast on. (Although your fabric is reversible, you will need to know which is the right side and which the wrong side when working shaping, etc.)

cable cast on

The cable cast on is a popular method of casting on that creates a firm edge. It can be a good cast on to use where an elastic, but sturdier, foundation row would be an advantage. Those with a standard to tight 'tension' like myself may find it more difficult to insert the knitting needle between the stitches and pull the yarn through, so make sure that you do not tighten up each new stitch on the left-hand needle too much. (See more about your knitting tension on page 34.)

1 Make a slip knot as shown previously. Then hold the knitting needle with the slip knot in your left hand and insert the right-hand needle from left to right and from front to back through the slip knot. Wrap the yarn from the ball up and over the point of the right-hand needle.

2 With the right-hand needle, draw a loop through the slip knot to make a new stitch. Do not drop the stitch from the left-hand needle, but instead slip the new stitch onto the left-hand needle as shown.

3 Then insert the right-hand needle between the two stitches on the left-hand needle and wrap the yarn around the point of the right-hand needle.

4 Pull the yarn through to make a new stitch and then place the new stitch on the left-hand needle as before. Repeat the last two steps to make the stitches you need.

29

knit and purl

After casting on stitches, you knit or purl them according to what your knitting pattern requires. The basic techniques for making knit or purl stitches are very simple and, once mastered, they are used to build up the knitted fabric.

the knit stitch

The knit stitch is the first stitch you will learn by following the steps below. When you have worked all the stitches from the left-hand needle onto the right-hand needle you have completed a 'row'. You then turn the work, transferring the needle with all the stitches to the left hand, and continue as before. When all stitches in all rows are knit stitches, it forms a reversible fabric called garter stitch. When purl rows are alternated with knit rows, it forms a fabric called stocking stitch, as shown below (on the 'right' side).

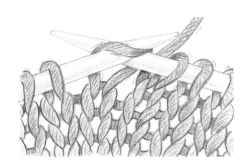
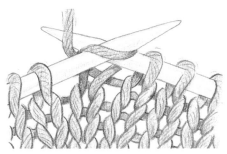
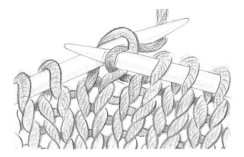

1 With the cast-on stitches on the needle in your left hand, insert the right-hand needle from left to right and from front to back through the first cast-on stitch.

2 Then take the yarn from the ball on your index finger (the working yarn) around the point of the right-hand needle.

3 Draw the right-hand needle and yarn through the stitch, forming a new stitch on the right-hand needle, and at the same time slip the original stitch off the left-hand needle. Repeat these steps until all the stitches from the left-hand needle have been worked. This is called a row.

the purl stitch

After the knit stitch, the next stitch to learn is the purl stitch. If every row is worked as a purl row, it creates the same fabric as if you had knitted every row garter stitch. Stocking stitch, alternating knit and purl rows (as shown below on the reverse side of the fabric), is the most commonly used knitted fabric. When working stocking stitch try to keep your tension consistent (see page 34) on both knit and purl rows. Uneven fabric is produced by working one side tighter or looser than the other, giving a 'stripy' effect.

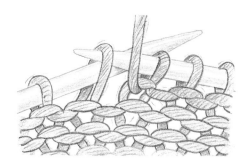

1 With the yarn to the front of the work, insert the right-hand needle from right to left into the front of the first stitch on the left-hand needle.

2 Then take the yarn from the ball on your index finger (the working yarn) around the point of the right-hand needle.

3 Draw the right-hand needle and the yarn through the stitch, thus forming a new stitch on the right-hand needle.

casting off

Casting off is the method used after you have completed your knitting to secure the stitches so they do not unravel. It is important that the cast-off edge is neither too tight nor too loose, and that it is elastic. This is particularly important when casting off on a neckband so that it can be pulled easily over the head. Casting off is also used to make

knit cast off

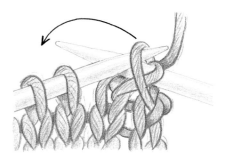 

1 Knit two stitches. Then insert the left-hand needle into the first stitch knitted on the right-hand needle and lift this stitch over the second stitch and off the right-hand needle.

2 One stitch is now on the right-hand needle. Knit the next stitch. Repeat the first step until all the stitches have been cast off. Then pull the yarn through the last stitch to fasten off.

most types of buttonholes and when more than one stitch needs to be decreased at once. Unless otherwise stated, cast off in the stitch pattern being used at that point, such as knitwise over a knit stitch and purlwise over a purl stitch.

purl cast off

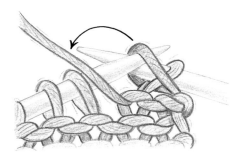

1 Purl two stitches. Insert the left-hand needle into the back of the first stitch worked on the right-hand needle and lift this stitch over the second stitch and off the right-hand needle.

2 One stitch is now on the right-hand needle. Purl the next stitch. Repeat the first step until all the stitches have been cast off. Then pull the yarn through the last stitch to fasten off.

tension

It is crucial to check your tension before you embark on a project. Tension is the number of stitches and rows to a centimetre or inch and is also known as stitch gauge. The tension determines the measurements of the garment so it is very important that you achieve the same tension as the designer. Don't be put off or swayed by experienced knitters who tell you that they never work a tension square, as they may have never questioned the strange proportions of their finished garment or why they needed more or less yarn than that quoted! A small difference over 10cm (4in) can add up to a considerable amount over the complete width of the knitted garment. However eager you are to start your project, take time to knit your tension square first: 15 minutes at that point can help to avoid disappointment later on.

measuring tension

Using the same yarn, needles and stitch pattern that is quoted in the section marked 'Tension' in your pattern, knit a sample at least 13cm (5in) square. Then smooth out the sample on a flat surface, but do not press it.

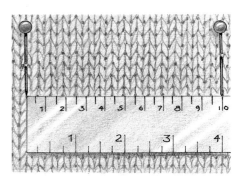

To check stitch tension, place a ruler or tape measure horizontally on the fabric and mark 10cm (4in) with pins. Count the number of stitches between the pins.
To check row tension, place a ruler or tape measure vertically, mark 10cm (4in) and count the number of rows.

● If the number of stitches and rows is greater than that stated in the pattern, your tension is too tight and your stitches are smaller than they should be. This can usually be remedied by changing to larger needles.

● If the number of stitches and rows is fewer than the specified number, your tension is looser and your stitches too large and you should try a smaller needle.

Obtaining the correct stitch tension is more important than the row tension as some patterns have the length worked in measurement, as in 'work until measures', and so the number of rows you need to work to obtain the length is less relevant. However, with some patterns, such as where motifs are worked over a certain number of rows, the row tension will still be very important.

The size of the knitted stitch depends on the yarn, the size of the knitting needles and your control of the yarn. It can also depend on mood – many knitters will have experienced a tighter tension when stress levels are high! A loose tension can produce an uneven, unstable fabric that can lose its shape, while a tight tension can create a hard, unelastic fabric. Your tension may change slightly from your sample when you are working over the larger number of stitches needed for the garment.

Your tension will also affect the amount of yarn you use. Some knitters may find that they always need a ball less or a ball more than that quoted. For instance, when I knitted the scarf on page 52, after I had achieved the length I wanted I had 38cm (15in) of yarn from my ball left. A tighter knitter, whose stitches are smaller, will need to knit more rows to achieve the same length and may need to go into a second ball of yarn to complete it.

increasing

To shape your knitting – for example, along armhole, neck and sleeve edges – there are various techniques for increasing or decreasing the number of stitches on your needle. The different methods for increasing are described overleaf.

Increases are worked to make your knitted fabric wider by adding to the number of stitches. They are most often used when shaping sleeves or after completing ribbing on the lower edges of backs, fronts and sleeves.

Increases can be used decoratively to add detailing to an otherwise plain design (see the Raglan cardigan with fully fashioned shaping on page 108). Decorative increases like this are placed two or three stitches from the edge of the knitting so they can be seen after the garment has been sewn up.

Increasing when working stocking stitch is relatively simple, but when working more complex stitch patterns, check to see if your instructions tell you to work extra increased stitches into the pattern.

Yarn-over increases are usually worked in lace patterns, followed by a decrease to create a hole or eyelet.

increase one ('inc one')

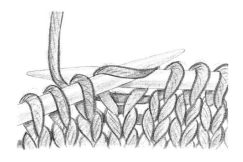

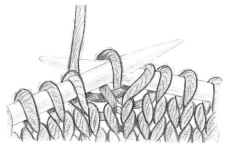

1 Insert the right-hand needle into the front of the next stitch, then knit the stitch but leave it on the left-hand needle.

2 Insert the right-hand needle into the back of the same stitch and knit it. Then slip the original stitch off the needle. You now have an extra stitch on the right-hand needle.

make one ('m1')

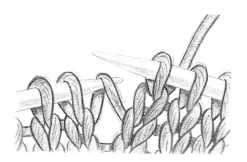

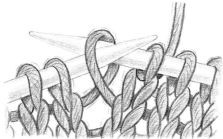

1 Insert the left-hand needle from front to back under the horizontal strand between the stitch just worked on the right-hand needle and the first stitch on the left-hand needle.

2 Knit into the back of the loop to twist it, thus preventing a hole. Then drop the strand from the left-hand needle. This forms a new stitch on the right-hand needle.

yarn over between a knit and a purl ('yrn')

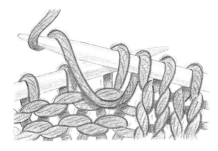

Bring the yarn forward between the two needles from the back to the front of the work, and take it over the top of the needle to the back again and then forward between the needles. Then purl the next stitch.

yarn over between purl stitches ('yrn')

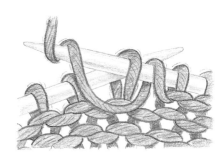

Bring the yarn over the needle to the back, then between the two needles to the front. Then purl the next stitch.

yarn over between a purl and a knit ('yon')

Take the yarn from the front over the needle to the back. Then knit the next stitch.

yarn over between knit stitches ('yf')

Bring the yarn forward between the two needles, from the back to the front of the work. Taking the yarn over the needle to do so, knit the next stitch.

decreasing

Decreases are used to make your fabric narrower by reducing the number of stitches. They are most often used when shaping necklines or the tops of sleeves. As with increases, decreases can form decorative detailing a few stitches from the edge, where different techniques are used to make the decreases slant to the right or left. This type of shaping, called 'fully fashioned', can be useful when shaping necks. By working 'knit 2 together' on the right neck edge and 'slip 1, knit 1, pass slipped stitch over' on the left side a neater edge is created, making it easier to pick up stitches around the neck for the neckband or collar. Worked one or two stitches in from the neckline edge, the slanting stitches can provide an interesting detail around the neck (see V-neck cardigan with contrast ribs on page 88).

**knit 2 together
('k2tog' or 'dec one')**

On a knit row, insert the right-hand needle from left to right through the next two stitches on the left-hand needle and knit them together. One stitch has been decreased.

purl 2 together ('p2tog' or 'dec one')

On a purl row, insert the right-hand needle from right to left through the next two stitches on the left-hand needle. Then purl them together. One stitch has been decreased.

slip 1, knit 1, pass slipped stitch over ('skpo')

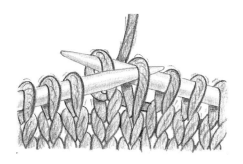

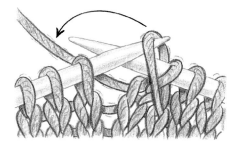

1 Insert the right-hand needle into the next stitch on the left-hand needle and slip it onto the right-hand needle without knitting it. Knit the next stitch. Then insert the left-hand needle into the slipped stitch as shown.

2 With the left-hand needle, lift the slipped stitch over the knitted stitch as shown and off the right-hand needle. One stitch has been decreased.

picking up stitches

'Picking up stitches' is a technique used when you need to knit a border directly onto a piece of knitting, for instance to add button bands on a cardigan or a neckband along a neck edge. To do this, you draw loops through the knitting with the tip of your knitting needle, forming stitches directly onto your needle.

Your knitting pattern will tell you how many stitches to pick up, and this should be done evenly. In the pattern, the instruction usually reads 'pick up and knit'.

along a selvedge (side edge)	**along a neck edge**
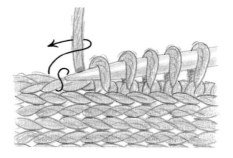	
With the right side of the knitting facing you, insert the knitting needle from front to back between the first and second stitches of the first row. Wrap the yarn around the needle and pull a loop through to form a new stitch on the needle. Continue in this way along the edge of the knitting.	On a neck edge, work along the straight edges as for a selvedge. But along the curved edges, insert the needle through the centre of the stitch below the shaping (to avoid large gaps) and pull a loop of yarn through to form a new stitch on the needle.

seams

The making up of a garment and adding picked-up borders is the last, but one of the most important, stages in producing a professional-looking garment. A beautifully knitted garment can be ruined by careless sewing up, or unevenly picked-up borders, as the knitter hurries to complete the project. So to avoid having a finish you won't be proud of, take a look at these basic techniques designed to help you perfect those finishing touches.

which stitch to use?

The seam that I use for almost all sewing up is mattress stitch, which produces a wonderfully invisible seam. It works well on any yarn and makes a completely straight seam as the same amount is taken up on each side – this also means that the knitted pieces should not need to be pinned together first. I find mattress stitch particularly invaluable when sewing seams on Fair Isle bands or striped pieces of knitting.

I use other types of seams less frequently, but they do have their uses. For instance, backstitch can sometimes be useful for sewing in a sleeve head, to neatly ease in the fullness. Just remember when using backstitch to sew up your knitting that it is important to ensure that you work in a completely straight line.

beginning a seam

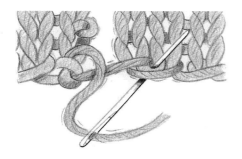

With the right sides of the knitting facing you and using the long tail left from your cast-on row, thread the strand into your blunt-ended sewing needle. Insert the sewing needle from back to front through the corner stitch of the other piece of knitting. Then make a figure of eight, and insert the needle from back to front into the stitch with the long tail. Pull the thread through to close the gap between the two pieces of knitting.

mattress stitch on stocking stitch

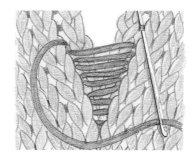

With the right sides of the knitting facing you, insert the needle under the horizontal bar between the first stitch and next stitch. Then insert the needle under the same bar on the other piece. Continue to do this, drawing up the thread to form the seam.

mattress stitch on garter stitch

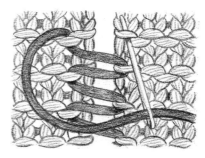

With the right sides of the knitting facing you, insert the needle through the bottom of the knot on the edge and then through the top of the corresponding knot on the opposite edge. Continue to do this from edge to edge, drawing up the thread to form a flat seam.

The seam for joining two cast-off edges is especially handy for shoulder seams, while the seam for joining a cast-off edge with a side edge (selvedge) is usually used when sewing a sleeve onto the body for a dropped shoulder style (see Boat neck sweater, page 68).

It is best to leave a long tail at the casting-on stage to sew up your knitting with, so that the sewing up yarn is already secured in place. If this is not possible, when first securing the thread for the seam, you should leave a length that can be darned in afterwards. All seams on knitting should be sewn with a large blunt-ended yarn or tapestry needle to avoid splitting the yarn.

rib seam – joining two knit-stitch edges

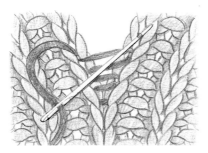

Insert the needle under a horizontal bar in the centre of a knit stitch at the edge of one piece of knitting and then at the edge of the other piece. Continue to do this, drawing up the thread to form one complete knit stitch along the seam.

rib seam – joining knit- and purl-stitch edges

Skip the purl stitch at the edge of one piece of knitting and join the seam at the centre of knit stitches, as for joining two knit-stitch edges.

**joining two cast-off
edges in stocking
stitch**

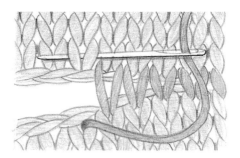 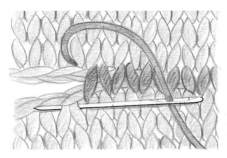

1 With the cast-off edges butted together, bring the needle out in the centre of the first stitch just below the cast-off edge on one piece. Insert the needle through the centre of the first stitch on the other piece and out through the centre of the next stitch.

2 Next, insert the needle through the centre of the first stitch on the first piece again and out through the centre of the stitch next to it. Continue in this way until the seam is completed.

**joining two cast-off
edges in garter stitch**

Insert needle under the two strands of a cast-off stitch on one edge and then under two strands of a cast-off stitch on the other edge. Continue in this way from edge to edge, drawing up the thread to form a flat seam.

**joining a cast-off edge
and a selvedge in
stocking stitch**

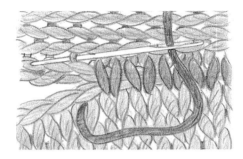

Bring the needle back to front through the centre of the first stitch on the cast-off edge. Then insert it under one or two horizontal strands between the first and second stitches on the selvedge and back through the centre of the same cast-off stitch. Pull up the thread so the seaming stitches disappear. Continue in this way until the seam is completed.

**joining a cast-off edge
and a selvedge in
garter stitch**

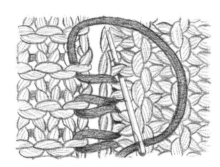

With the right sides of the knitting facing you, insert the needle under the top of one stitch on the selvedge or row end edge and then under the two strands of a single cast-off stitch on the opposite edge. Continue to do this from edge to edge, drawing up the thread to form an invisible seam.

darning in ends

You will always have some ends to darn in, even on one-colour projects – where you start a new ball of yarn, for instance. Ends can be darned in or sewn vertically and horizontally.

Thread the loose end onto a blunt-ended needle and run it over and under the horizontal bars of the stitches at the back of the work. Ends can also be darned in vertically along the edge of the pieces after seaming.

fixing mistakes

A dropped or incorrect stitch is a common mistake. Depending on the type of stitch dropped or when the mistake occurred, you can pick up, unpick or unravel using the methods introduced here.

picking up a knit stitch on the row below

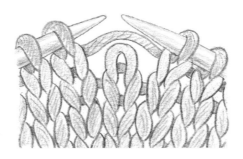

1 A dropped stitch.

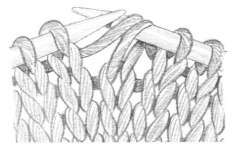

2 Working from front to back, pick up the stitch and the horizontal strand above it with the right-hand needle (the strand should be behind the stitch).

picking up a stitch several rows below

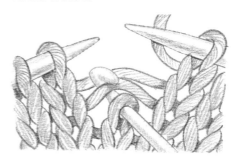

The dropped stitch forms a ladder running down a number of rows and can be picked up with a crochet hook. Always work from the front – or knit side – of the fabric. Insert the hook into the free stitch from the front. With the hook pointing upwards, catch the first strand of the ladder from above and draw it through the stitch. Continue in this way until all the strands have been worked, then replace the stitch on the left-hand needle, taking care not to twist it. If more than one stitch has been dropped, secure the others with a safety pin until you are ready to pick them up.

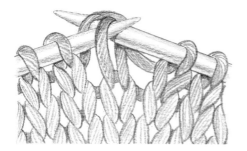

3 Insert the left-hand needle through the back of the stitch and lift it over the strand and off the needle as though casting off.

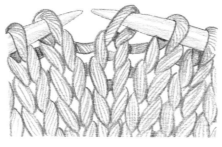

4 The stitch is made facing the wrong way. Insert the left-hand needle through the front of the stitch and slip it onto the needle. The stitch is then in the right position.

baby knits patterns

garter stitch scarf

The first project is a garter stitch scarf. Not only will this be probably the easiest piece you will ever knit, but you can relax and enjoy creating your first fabric while gaining grounding in the fundamentals of casting on and off, the knit stitch and tension. If you knit every stitch and every row it creates a reversible fabric called garter stitch. You can recognise it by the wavy horizontal ridges it creates.

Normally at this stage you should knit a tension square to make sure your tension is the same as that quoted in the pattern before you start the project, but as this item is basically a narrow strip you can begin to work the scarf straight away.

techniques focus
(casting on and (overleaf) the knit stitch and casting off (see also pages 26–7, 30 and 32)

casting on

1 Make a slip knot, leaving a long tail. With the slip knot on the needle in your right hand and the yarn that comes from the ball over your index finger, wrap the tail end of the yarn over your left thumb from front to back. Secure the yarn in your left palm with your fingers.

2 Then insert the knitting needle upwards through the yarn loop on your left thumb.

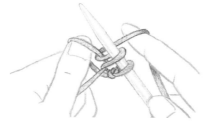

3 Next, with the right index finger, wrap the yarn from the ball up and over the point of the knitting needle.

4 Then draw the yarn through the loop on your thumb to form a new stitch on the knitting needle. Lastly, let the yarn loop slip off your left thumb and pull the loose end to tighten up the stitch. Repeat these steps to make the stitches you need.

Cast on the number of stitches quoted in the pattern and knit for approximately 10cm (4in). Lay the work down on a flat surface and put a ruler or tape measure across the width. If the piece of knitting measures 12cm (4¾in) across then you will know that your tension is correct as it is the same as that quoted in the pattern. You can then carry on knitting until you achieve the length needed. If it is wider, then your tension is looser and you are creating larger stitches; if it is narrower, your tension is tighter and you are creating smaller stitches. On a small piece such as a scarf this may not be significant

the knit stitch

1 With the cast-on stitches on the needle in your left hand, insert the right-hand needle from left to right and simultaneously from front to back through the first cast-on stitch.

2 Then take the yarn from the ball on your index finger (the working yarn) around the point of the right-hand needle.

3 Draw the right-hand needle and yarn through the stitch, thus forming a new stitch on the right-hand needle, and at the same time slip the original stitch off the left-hand needle. Repeat these steps until all the stitches from the left-hand needle have been worked. This is called a row.

enough for you to feel you need to change needle sizes but on any other pattern you should do so, as your garment will be larger or smaller than it should be (see Tension on page 34).

Measuring tension over garter stitch is different from over stocking stitch as it is a unique stitch pattern where the rows compress so that it takes two rows to create the distinctive wavy garter stitch ridge. To count the number of rows, count the ridges and multiply by two.

knit cast off

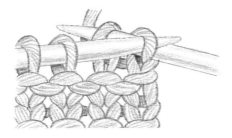 

1 Knit two stitches. Then insert the left-hand needle into the first stitch knitted on the right-hand needle and lift this stitch over the second stitch and off the right-hand needle.

2 One stitch is now on the right-hand needle. Knit the next stitch. Repeat the first step until all the stitches have been cast off. Then pull the yarn through the last stitch to fasten off.

garter stitch scarf

measurements
Approximately 12 x 55cm/4¾ x 21¾in

materials
One 50g ball Debbie Bliss cashmerino aran in Pale Pink.
Pair of 5mm (US 8) knitting needles.

tension
18 sts and 38 rows to 10cm/4in square over garter st with 5mm (US 8) needles.

abbreviations
cm = centimetre(s) **in** = inch(es) **K(k)** = knit **mm** = millimetres **st(s)** = stitch(es)

to make
With 5mm (US 8) needles, cast on 22 sts.
Garter stitch row K all sts.
Repeat this row until you have approximately 38cm/15in of yarn remaining.
Cast off.
Darn in the yarn ends.

garter stitch blanket

A soft blanket in a cashmere mix is the perfect way to envelop a small baby. By working the squares in different shades you can create a patchwork of colour without having to worry about tackling complicated colour techniques.

As with the scarf, tension is not as important as it usually is, as any alteration made in measurements won't be a problem on a blanket because it does not need to fit a particular size. However, with this pattern you are now being introduced to another knitting essential, seaming.

How you sew up your project (often called finishing) is almost as important as the quality of your knitting. Just as an uneven fabric can spoil your finished work, so badly sewn-up seams can make a beautifully knitted design look poorly made. Try to use the yarn you have been knitting with to sew up your seams but if you have been using a fancy, textured yarn or one that breaks easily, substitute a smooth yarn in a matching shade. Textured yarns get caught up and knotted all too easily. Use a blunt-ended embroidery or darning needle as a sharp point can split the yarn.

As garter stitch can sometimes stretch, the squares have been sewn together alternating the direction of the garter stitch, thereby sewing cast-on or cast-off rows to row ends.

The most challenging part of this project is sewing in the ends of yarn where you have started or finished each square. The technique is easy but on a blanket with individual squares it will be time consuming. Allow yourself plenty of time and a comfortable chair with good back support.

techniques focus
seams (see also page 47)

darning in ends

joining a cast-off edge and a selvedge in garter stitch

Thread the loose end onto a blunt-ended needle and run it over and under the horizontal bars of the stitches at the back of the work. Ends can also be darned in vertically along the edge of the pieces after seaming.

With the right sides of the knitting facing you, insert the needle under the top of one stitch on the selvedge or row end edge and then under the two strands of a single cast-off stitch on the opposite edge. Continue to do this from edge to edge, drawing up the thread as you work to form an invisible seam.

garter stitch blanket

measurements	Approximately 49 x 56cm/19¼ x 22in
materials	One 50g ball Debbie Bliss cashmerino aran in each of Pale Mauve (A), Fuchsia (B), Teal (D) and Dark Mauve (E), and two 50g balls in Pale Blue (C). Pair of 5mm (US 8) knitting needles. Large blunt-ended embroidery or darning needle.
tension	18 sts and 38 rows to 10cm/4in square over garter st on 5mm (US 8) needles.
abbreviations	**cm** = centimetre(s) **in** = inch(es) **K(k)** = knit **mm** = millimetres **st(s)** = stitch(es)
garter stitch squares	With 5mm (US 8) needles, cast on 14 sts. K 24 rows. Cast off.
blanket	Make 56 squares, 11 in A, 9 in B, 14 in C, 11 in D and 11 in E. Assemble the squares as shown in the diagram, turning every alternate square through 90°, so that cast-on and cast-off edges join onto row ends.

A	B	C	E	D	C	E
C	A	D	B	C	D	A
B	D	A	C	E	A	E
E	C	B	E	B	C	D
C	A	E	C	D	A	B
E	D	C	B	A	D	C
D	A	D	C	E	A	D
C	B	E	A	C	B	E

sachets

These sachets can be filled with sweet-smelling lavender or, more practically, cotton wool balls and other such baby essentials.

The stitch pattern you are using here is the most common one used in knitting, stocking stitch. Stocking stitch is constructed from alternating rows of knit stitches and purl stitches. Unlike garter stitch, it is not reversible as the front and back of the work look quite different, with the stitches on the front of the work forming small Vs.

The back of the work will look more like garter stitch, and is called reverse stocking stitch. Generally the knit row is considered the right side of the fabric and will be called this in the pattern and the purl row will be called the wrong side. Knit and purl stitches can also be used within the same row to create other patterns, such as rib and moss stitch (see Cushions with buttonholes, page 76).

This project is a good one to practise measuring your tension over stocking stitch. When you have finished the strip of knitting, lay it out flat and measure the tension following the diagram overleaf.

purl stitch

 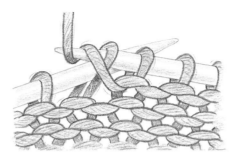 

1 With the yarn to the front of the work, insert the right-hand needle from right to left into the front of the first stitch on the left-hand needle.

2 Then take the yarn from the ball on your index finger (the working yarn) around the point of the right-hand needle.

2 Draw the right-hand needle and the yarn through the stitch, thus forming a new stitch on the right-hand needle.

techniques focus
purl stitch (above) and
tension and seams
(see also pages 31, 34
and 44)

tension

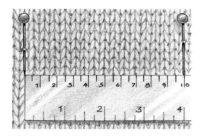

To check stitch tension, place a ruler or tape measure horizontally on the fabric and mark 10cm (4in) with pins. Count the number of stitches between the pins.

To check row tension, place a ruler or tape measure vertically, mark 10cm (4in) and count the number of rows.

mattress stitch on stocking stitch

With the right sides of the knitting facing you, insert the needle under the horizontal bar between the first stitch and next stitch. Then insert the needle under the same bar on the other piece. Continue to do this, drawing up the thread to form the seam.

sachets

measurements

Approximately 15 x 15cm/6 x 6in

materials

One 50g ball Debbie Bliss cotton double knitting.
Pair of 4mm (US 6) knitting needles.
1 button.
51cm/20in of narrow satin ribbon.

tension

20 sts and 28 rows to 10cm/4in square over st st using 4mm (US 6) needles.

abbreviations

cm = centimetre(s) **cont** = continue **in** = inch(es) **K(k)** = knit **mm** = millimetres
P(p) = purl **rep** = repeat **st(s)** = stitch(es) **st st** = stocking stitch

to make

With 4mm (US 6) needles, cast on 30 sts.
1st row (right side) K all sts.
2nd row (wrong side) P all sts.
These 2 rows are repeated to form st st.
Cont in st st until work measures 40cm/16in from cast-on edge, ending with a 1st row.
Cast off all sts knitwise.

to make up

Sew a button, centrally to the right side of the knitting, 13cm/5½in above the cast-on edge.
Fold the knitting so that the cast-on edge is 10cm/4in below the cast-off edge. Join the
side seams as described opposite to form an envelope. Thread the ribbon through the
centre of the cast-off edge and tie. Fold the flap over the front and wind the ribbon around
the button to hold the sachet closed.

boat neck sweater

This pattern introduces you to shaping, which makes a garment fit better or makes it more practical to wear. In this design straight sleeves that measured the same all the way up would produce a piece that fitted comfortably at the top but would be too wide at the wrist. So here they are made wider at the top than the bottom by adding more stitches at the beginning and end of certain rows. This technique is called increasing.

The style of sleeve used here is called a dropped shoulder: the straight cast-off edge is sewn to the body without armhole shaping. When sewing on the sleeves measure the top of the sleeve and place the centre of the cast-off edge to the shoulder seam. Pin the beginning and end of the row to the back and front at the same distance from the shoulder seam. Sew together the shoulders using cast-off rows of garter stitch.

techniques focus
increasing and (overleaf) seams (see also pages 36 and 46–7)

increase one ('inc one')

 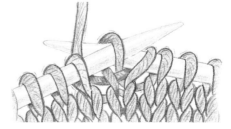

1 Insert the the right-hand needle into the front of the next stitch, then knit the stitch but leave it on the left-hand needle.

2 Insert the right-hand needle into the back of the same stitch and knit it. Then slip the original stitch off the needle. You now have an extra stitch on the right-hand needle.

joining two cast-off edges in garter stitch

Insert needle under the two strands of a cast-off stitch on one edge and then under two strands of a cast-off stitch on the other edge. Continue in this way from edge to edge, drawing up the thread to form a flat seam.

joining a cast-off edge and a selvedge in stocking stitch

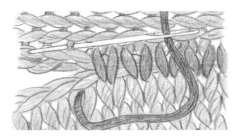

Bring the needle back to front through the centre of the first stitch on the cast-off edge. Then insert it under one or two horizontal strands between the first and second stitches on the selvedge and back through the centre of the same cast-off stitch. Pull up the thread so the seaming stitches disappear. Continue in this way until the seam is completed.

boat neck sweater

measurements	To fit ages	0–3	3–6	6–9	9–12	months
	Actual measurements					
	Chest	48	52	56	61	cm
		19	20½	22	24	in
	Length to shoulder	22	24	26	28	cm
		8¾	9½	10¼	11	in
	Sleeve length	14	16	18	20	cm
		5½	6¼	7	8	in

materials
2(3:3:4) 50g balls Debbie Bliss cashmerino aran in Lilac.
Pair each of 4½mm (US 7) and 5mm (US 8) knitting needles.

tension
18 sts and 24 rows to 10cm/4in square over st st using 5mm (US 8) needles.

abbreviations
beg = beginning **cm** = centimetre(s) **cont** = continue **foll** = following **in** = inch(es)
inc = increase one st by working into front and back of stitch **K(k)** = knit
mm = millimetres **P(p)** = purl **st(s)** = stitch(es) **st st** = stocking stitch

**back and front
(both alike)**

With 4½mm (US 7) needles, cast on 45(49:53:57) sts.
K 2 rows.
Change to 5mm (US 8) needles.
Beg with a k row, work in st st until work measures 22(24:26:28)cm/8¾(9½:10¼:11)in, ending with a p row.
K 2 rows.
Cast off all sts knitwise.

sleeves

With 4½mm (US 7) needles, cast on 30(32:34:36) sts.
K 2 rows.
Change to 5mm (US 8) needles.
Beg with a k row, work 2 rows in st st.
Inc row (right side) Inc one st, k to last st, inc one st.
Beg with a p row, work 5 rows in st st.
Cont in st st and inc as before on next and every foll 6th row until there are 40(44:48:52) sts.
Cont straight until sleeve measures 14(16:18:20)cm/5½(6¼:7:8)in from cast-on edge, ending with a p row.
Cast off.

to make up

Join front to back at shoulders, leaving 17(18:18:19)cm/6¾(7:7:7½)in open in centre for neck. Sew on sleeves. Join side and sleeve seams.

simple hat

This simple hat is the ideal way to practise decreasing, the next stage in learning shaping. Decreasings are used when you want to get rid of stitches and are usually found when you need to add shape at the edges of a garment or in the centre of your knitting, as in necklines.

The hat is knitted in stocking stitch, with a gentle roll round the rim, so make sure your cast on is fairly loose; the best way to do this is by using the thumb method (page 26). If it is too tight, it will be difficult to get on the baby's head. Where the hat rolls up at the bottom, reverse the seam for a neater look.

technique focus
decreasing (see also page 40)

knit 2 together ('k2tog' or 'dec one')

On a knit row, insert the right-hand needle from left to right through the next two stitches on the left-hand needle and knit them together. One stitch has been decreased.

simple hat

sizes	**To fit ages** 3–6 6–12 months
materials	Two 50g balls Debbie Bliss double knitting cotton in Lilac. Pair of 4mm (US 6) knitting needles.
tension	20 sts and 28 rows to 10cm/4in square over st st using 4mm (US 6) needles.
abbreviations	**beg** = beginning **cm** = centimetre(s) **dec** = decrease **in(s)** = inch(es) **K(k)** = knit **P(p)** = purl **rem** = remaining **st(s)** = stitch(es) **st st** = stocking stitch **tog** = together
to make	With 4mm (US 6) needles, cast on 73(82) sts. Beg with a k row, work 40 rows in st st. **Dec row** K1, [k2tog, k7] 8(9) times. 65(73) sts. P 1 row. **Dec row** K1, [k2tog, k6] 8(9) times. 57(64) sts. P 1 row. **Dec row** K1, [k2tog, k5] 8(9) times. 49(55) sts. P 1 row. **Dec row** K1, [k2tog, k4] 8(9) times. 41(46) sts. P 1 row. **Dec row** K1, [k2tog, k3] 8(9) times. 33(37) sts. P 1 row. **Dec row** K1, [k2tog, k2] 8(9) times. 25(28) sts. P 1 row. **Next row** K1(0), [k2tog] to end. 13(14) sts. P 1 row. **Next row** K1(0), [k2tog] to end. 7 sts. Beg with a p row, work 11 rows in st st. Break yarn leaving approximately 40cm/16in, thread through rem 7 sts, pull up and secure. Join seam, reversing seam on lower 2cm/¾in for the roll of the hem.

cushions with buttonholes

The cushions introduce you not only to buttonholes but also to two of my favourite stitch patterns, moss stitch (or seed stitch) and rib. Moss stitch is a beautiful pattern that is perfect as an all-over fabric but also is a great alternative to rib on welts or collars. It can be time-consuming as the yarn is passed backwards and forwards between each stitch but it is well worth the effort.

The buttonhole on this cushion is the easiest of all and is created by bringing the yarn forward from the back of the work to the front and then knitting two stitches together. By making a stitch and losing a stitch in this way, a hole is created on one row but the number of stitches on the needle remains the same.

It is good to use on thicker yarns where a decent-sized buttonhole can be made with very little effort. On finer yarns it can make too small a hole. The larger buttonhole is made by casting off stitches on one row and then turning the work and casting on the same number of stitches on the second row. The number of stitches you cast on and off depends on the size of the hole you want and how thick your yarn is.

Rib stitches are usually used to pull in fabric, such as on the lower edges of garments,

neckbands or sleeve cuffs. The rib used in this cushion is particularly good to work as by purling the second, wrong side row, it prevents the fabric pulling in too much. It also makes it quicker to knit! The tension on rib is sometimes quoted on patterns when the fabric is slightly stretched out or after light pressing.

techniques focus
increasing (see also page 40)

yarn over between knit stitches ('yf')

Bring the yarn forward between the two needles, from the back to the front of the work. Taking the yarn over the needle to do so, knit the next stitch.

making a cast-off buttonhole

On the first buttonhole row, work to the buttonhole position, cast off the number of stitches required, then carry on to the end of the row. On the second row, work to the cast-off stitches, turn your work around so that the right side is facing and, using the cable method, cast on the same number of stitches on your left-hand needle that you had cast off. Turn the work back again, and work to end of the row.

moss stitch cushion

measurements   25 x 25cm/10 x 10in

materials   Four 50g balls Debbie Bliss merino chunky in Ecru.
Pair of 6½mm (US 10½) knitting needles.
3 buttons.
25 x 25cm/10 x 10in cushion pad.

tension   14 sts and 24 rows to 10cm/4in square over moss st using 6½mm (US 10½) needles.

abbreviations   **cm** = centimetre(s) **in** = inch(es) **K(k)** = knit **mm** = millimetres **patt** = pattern
P(p) = purl **rep** = repeat **st(s)** = stitch(es) **tog** = together **yf** = yarn forward

to make   With 6½mm (US 10½) needles, cast on 37 sts.
Moss st row P1, * k1, p1; rep from * to end.
Rep this row until work measures 56cm/22in.
Buttonhole row [P1, k1] 3 times, * yf, k2tog, [p1, k1] 5 times; rep from * once more, yf,
k2tog, [p1,k1] twice, p1.
Work a further 2cm/¾in in moss st.
Cast off.

to make up   Fold cushion so that cast-on edge is 10cm/4in below cast-off edge. Join side seams.
Sew buttons to the right side, 5cm/2in below cast-on edge to correspond with
buttonholes. Turn to right side, insert cushion pad and fasten buttons.

ribbed cushion

measurements   25 x 25cm/10 x 10in

materials   Three 50g balls Debbie Bliss merino chunky in Pale Blue.
Pair of 6½mm (US 10½) knitting needles.
3 buttons.
25 x 25cm/10 x 10in cushion pad.

tension   14 sts and 18 rows to 10cm/4in square over rib patt using 6½mm (US 10½) needles.

abbreviations   **cm** = centimetre(s) **in** = inch(es) **K(k)** = knit **mm** = millimetres **patt** = pattern
P(p) = purl **rep** = repeat **st(s)** = stitch(es)

to make   With 6½mm (US 10½) needles, cast on 37 sts.
1st row (right side) K2, [p1, k3] 8 times, p1, k2.
2nd row P to end.
Rep the last 2 rows until work measures 52cm/20½in from cast-on edge, ending with a wrong side row.
Buttonhole row (right side) K2, p1, [k2, cast off 2 sts, k next 2 sts, p1, k3, p1] twice, k2, cast off 2 sts, k next 2 sts, p1, k2.
Next row P6, [cast on 2 sts, p10] twice, cast on 2 sts, p5.
Patt 1 row.
Cast off knitwise.

to make up   Fold work in half and join side seams. Sew buttons to inside of cushion back to match buttonholes. Insert cushion pad and fasten buttons.

jacket with moss stitch bands

This neat little cardigan has button and buttonhole bands that are worked in one piece with the fronts. This means that you do not have to pick up stitches along the front edges. As there is a shaped neckline, stitches do need to be picked up across the front bands, up the right side neck, across the back neck stitches and down the left front neck to work the neckband.

The moss stitch borders on the hem of the cardigan sleeve cuffs and neckband are knitted on smaller needles to make a neater edge. Moss stitch is one of my favourite stitches for edgings and is a pretty alternative to ribbed edgings.

technique focus
picking up stitches (see also page 42)

along a selvedge (side edge)

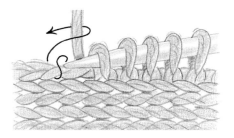

With the right side of the knitting facing you, insert the knitting needle from front to back between the first and second stitches of the first row. Wrap the yarn around the needle and pull a loop through to form a new stitch on the needle. Continue working in this way along the edge of the knitting.

along a neck edge

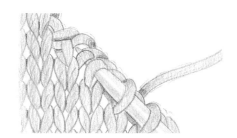

On a neck edge, work along the straight edges as for a selvedge. But along the curved edges, insert the needle through the centre of the stitch below the shaping (to avoid large gaps) and pull a loop of yarn through to form a new stitch on the needle.

jacket with moss stitch bands

measurements

To fit ages	0–3	3–6	6–9	9–12	12–24	24–36	months
Actual measurements							
Chest	48	52	56	60	65	70	cm
	19	20½	22	23½	25¾	27½	in
Length to shoulder	21	24	26	28	32	36	cm
	8¼	9½	10¼	11	12½	14¼	in
Sleeve length	13	15	17	19	22	24	cm
	5	6	6¾	7½	8¾	9½	in

materials

2(3:3:3:4:5) 50g balls of Debbie Bliss baby cashmerino in Pale Pink.
Pair each of 3mm (US 2) and 3¼mm (US 3) knitting needles.
6(6:6:6:7:7) buttons.

tension

25 sts and 34 rows to 10cm/4in square over st st using 3¼mm (US 3) needles.

abbreviations

beg = beginning **cm** = centimetre(s) **cont** = continue **dec** = decrease **foll** = following
in = inch(es) **inc** = increase one st by working into front and back of st **K(k)** = knit
mm = millimetres **P(p)** = purl **rem** = remaining **rep** = repeat **st(s)** = stitch(es)
st st = stocking stitch **tog** = together **yf** = yarn forward

back

With 3mm (US 2) needles, cast on 61(67:71:75:83:87) sts.
Moss st row K1, * p1, k1; rep from * to end.
This row forms moss st.
Rep the last row 5 times more.
Change to 3¼mm (US 3) needles.
Beg with a k row, work in st st until back measures 21(24:26:28:32:36)cm/
8¼(9½:10¼:11:12½:14¼)in from cast-on edge, ending with a p row.
Shape shoulders
Cast off 17(19:20:21:23:24) sts at beg of next 2 rows.
Leave rem 27(29:31:33:37:39) sts on a spare needle.

left front

With 3mm (US 2) needles, cast on 35(39:41:43:47:49) sts.
Moss st row P1, * k1, p1; rep from * to end.
This row forms moss st.
Rep the last row 5 times more.
Change to 3¼mm (US 3) needles.
Next row (right side) K to last 6 sts, moss st 6.
Next row Moss st 6, p to end.
Rep the last 2 rows 22(27:32:32:39:45) times more.
Shape neck
Next row K to last 9(10:11:11:11:12) sts, leave these sts on a stitch holder.
Dec one st at neck edge on every row until 17(19:20:21:23:24) sts rem.
Cont straight until front measures same as back to shoulder, ending at armhole edge.
Shape shoulder
Cast off.

right front

With 3mm (US 2) needles, cast on 35(39:41:43:47:49) sts.
Moss st row P1, * k1, p1; rep from * to end.
This row forms moss st.
Rep the last row 3 times more.
Next row (buttonhole row) P1, k1, p1, k2tog, yf, moss st to end.
Next row Moss st to end.
Change to 3¼mm (US 3) needles.
Next row (right side) Moss st 6, k to end.
Next row P to last 6 sts, moss st 6.
Rep the last 2 rows 3(4:5:5:5:6) times more.
Next row (buttonhole row) P1, k1, p1, k2tog, yf, k to end.
Next row P to last 6 sts, moss st 6.
Rep the last 10(12:14:14:14:16) rows 3(3:3:3:4:4) times more.
Next row Moss st 6, k to end.
Next row P to last 6 sts, moss st 6.
Rep the last 2 rows 2(3:4:4:4:5) times more.
Shape neck
Next row Moss st 6 sts, then k3(4:5:5:5:6) sts, leave these 9(10:11:11:11:12) sts on a stitch holder, k to end.
Dec one st at neck edge on every row until 17(19:20:21:23:24) sts rem.
Cont straight until front measures same as back to shoulder, ending at armhole edge.
Shape shoulder
Cast off.

sleeves

With 3mm (US 2) needles, cast on 25(29:33:35:37:39) sts.
Moss st row P1, * k1, p1; rep from * to end.
This row forms moss st.
Rep the last row 5 times more.
Change to 3¼mm (US 3) needles.
Beg with a k row, work in st st and inc one st at each end of the 3rd and every foll 4th row until there are 47(51:57:63:71:79) sts.
Cont straight until sleeve measures 13(15:17:19:22:24)cm/5(6:6¾:7½:8¾:9½)in from cast-on edge, ending with a p row.
Cast off.

neckband

Join shoulder seams.
With right side facing and 3mm (US 2) needles, slip 9(10:11:11:11:12) sts from right front neck holder onto a needle, pick up and k16(16:17:17:18:18) sts up right front neck, k27(29:31:33:35:37) sts from back neck holder, pick up and k16(16:17:17:18:18) sts down left front neck, k3(4:5:5:5:6) sts, then moss st 6 from left front holder.
77(81:87:89:93:97) sts.
Work 1 row in moss st.
Next row (buttonhole row) P1, k1, p1, k2tog, yf, moss st to end.
Work 3 rows in moss st.
Cast off in moss st.

to make up

Matching centre of cast-off edge of sleeve to shoulder, sew on sleeves. Join side and sleeve seams. Sew on buttons.

v-neck cardigan with contrast ribs

Often front bands such as buttonbands are worked after the garment has been completed. This is because stitches such as ribs need to be worked on a smaller needle to create the neatest finish. There are two main types of front bands: one where the band is knitted and sewn on separately, and the other where stitches are picked up down the front edges. I prefer the latter as a sewn-on band can look messy.

The rib pattern is created by alternating knit and purl stitches in the same row and is often used on edgings as its elasticity means it stretches over the head and hands and then springs back into shape. The most commonly used combinations are k1, p1 ribbing, known as single rib, and k2, p2 ribbing, known as double rib.

techniques focus
increasing and (overleaf) seams (see also pages 37 and 43–5)

make 1 ('m 1')

1 Insert the left-hand needle from front to back under the horizontal strand between the stitch just worked on the right-hand needle and the first stitch on the left-hand needle.

2 Knit into the back of the loop to twist it, thus preventing a hole. Then drop the strand from the left-hand needle. This forms a new stitch on the right-hand needle.

knit 2 together through back of loop ('k2 tog tbl')

Knit into the back loop of the stitch instead of the front. This is called knit through back of loop (k1 tbl). In k2 tog tbl you knit both stitches together through the back of the loop.

In this design, the ribs are in a contrasting colour to make it easier for you to see the new stitch you are creating when you pick up the stitches. When changing colour on moving from rib to stocking stitch at the bottom of the body and sleeves, cut the contrast thread, leaving a long enough end to ensure the first stitch does not unravel later and that there is enough yarn to darn in afterwards. Begin working in stocking stitch with the main shade, again making sure you have left an end of at least 8cm (3½in). The decreasing on the neck is worked one stitch in from the edge. This is called fully fashioned decreasing and the slanting stitch creates decorative interest. When decreasing in from the edge, you can pick up and knit your stitches following the technique for a straight edge rather than a curved edge.

v-neck cardigan with contrast ribs

measurements	To fit ages	3–6	6–9	9–12	months
	Actual measurements				
	Chest	52	56	61	cm
		20½	22	24	in
	Length to shoulder	24	26	28	cm
		9½	10¼	11	in
	Sleeve length	14	16	18	cm
		5½	6¼	7	in

materials

3(4:4) 50g balls Debbie Bliss cotton double knitting in Lilac (M) and one ball in Fuchsia (C).
Pair each of 3¾mm (US 5) and 4mm (US 6) knitting needles.
4 buttons.

tension

20 sts and 28 rows to 10cm/4in square over st st using 4mm (US 6) needles.

abbreviations

beg = beginning **cm** = centimetre(s) **cont** = continue **foll** = following **in** = inch(es)
inc = increase **K(k)** = knit **m1** = make 1 **mm** = millimetres **P(p)** = purl
rem = remaining **rep** = repeat **st(s)** = stitch(es) **st st** = stocking stitch
tbl = through back loop **tog** = together **yrn** = yarn round needle

back

With 4mm (US 6) needles and C, cast on 54(58:62) sts.
1st row (right side) K0(2:0), * p2, k2; rep from * to last 2(0:2) sts, p2(0:2).
2nd row P0(2:0), * k2, p2; rep from * to last 2(0:2) sts, k2(0:2).
Rep these 2 rows once more.
Change to M.
Beg with a k row, work in st st until back measures 24(26:28)cm/9½(10¼:11)in, ending with a p row.
Shape shoulders
Cast off 18(18:20) sts at beg of next 2 rows.
Leave rem 18(22:22) sts on a stitch holder.

left front

With 4mm (US 6) needles and C, cast on 25(27:29) sts.
1st row (right side) K0(2:0), * p2, k2; rep from * to last 5 sts, p2, k3.
2nd row P3, * k2, p2; rep from * to last 2(0:2) sts, k2(0:2).
Rep these 2 rows once more.
Change to M.
1st and 2nd sizes only
K 1 row.
3rd size only
Inc row (right side) K7, m1, k to last 7 sts, m1, k7. 31 sts.
All sizes
Beg with a p row, work in st st until front measures 17(18:19)cm/6¾(7:7½)in, ending with a p row.
Shape neck
Next row (right side) K to last 3 sts, k2tog, k1.
P 1 row.
Rep the last 2 rows 6(8:10) times more. 18(18:20) sts.
Work straight until front measures same as back to shoulder, ending with a p row.
Cast off.

right front

With 4mm (US 6) needles and C, cast on 25(27:29) sts.
1st row (right side) K3, * p2, k2; rep from * to last 2(0:2) sts, p2(0:2).
2nd row P0(2:0), * k2, p2; rep from * to last 5 sts, k2, p3.
Rep these 2 rows once more.
Change to M.
1st and 2nd sizes only
K 1 row.
3rd size only
Inc row (right side) K7, m1, k to last 7 sts, m1, k7. 31 sts.
All sizes
Beg with a p row, work in st st until front measures 17(18:19)cm/6¾(7:7½)in, ending with a p row.
Shape neck
Next row (right side) K1, k2tog tbl, k to end.
P 1 row.
Rep the last 2 rows 6(8:10) times more. 18(18:20) sts.
Work straight until front measures same as back to shoulder, ending with a k row.
Cast off.

sleeves

With 4mm (US 6) needles and C, cast on 30(30:34) sts.
1st row (right side) K2, * p2, k2; rep from * to end.
2nd row P2, * k2, p2; rep from * to end.
Rep these 2 rows once more.
Change to M.
Beg with a k row, work 4 rows in st st.
Inc row (right side) K2, m1, k to last 2 sts, m1, k2.
Beg with a p row, work 3 rows in st st.
Cont in st st and inc as before on next and every foll 4th row until there are 42(46:50) sts.
Cont straight until sleeve measures 14(16:18)cm/5½(6¼:7)in from cast-on edge, ending with a p row.
Cast off.

front edging

Join shoulder seams.

With right side facing, 3¾mm (US 5) needles and C, pick up and k 30(32:34) sts along right front edge from cast-on edge to start of neck shaping, 24(26:28) sts up right front neck to shoulder, k across 18(22:22) sts from back neck stitch holder, pick up and k 24(26:28) sts down left front neck to start of neck shaping and 30(32:34) sts along left front edge to cast-on edge. 126(138:146) sts.

1st row (wrong side) P2, * k2, p2; rep from * to end.

Buttonhole row K2, yrn, p2tog, rib 6(6:8), [yrn, rib 2tog, rib 6(8:8)] once more, yrn, rib 2tog, rib to end.

3rd row As 1st row.

4th row K2, * p2, k2; rep from * to end.

Cast off in rib.

to make up

Matching centre of cast-off edge of sleeve to shoulder, sew on sleeves. Join side and sleeve seams.

moss stitch shoes

One of the nicest baby gifts to make is a tiny pair of shoes or bootees as they always look really appealing. To make them even more special they can always be decorated after knitting with ribbon or embroidery.

These moss stitch shoes have a relatively simple pattern, using casting on and off and increases and decreases to create the shape. When adding or losing stitches in a pattern, such as moss stitch, you need to keep the pattern consistent. In moss stitch, for instance, on every row you work a knit stitch over the knit stitch from the previous row and a purl stitch over a purl stitch. If you then make a mistake and work a knit over a purl stitch, your moss stitch will become rib. To practise working moss stitch and understanding how to keep the pattern consistent, try knitting these two swatches on larger needles and thicker yarn such as double knitting on 4mm (US 6) needles. This is known as keeping the continuity of the pattern or keeping the pattern correct.

technique focus
moss stitch

On one swatch cast on an even number of stitches and work the pattern as follows:
1st row K1[p1, k1] to end.
2nd row P1[k1, p1] to end.
Repeat these 2 rows until you have worked a square. Cast off.

On the other swatch cast on an uneven number of stitches and work the pattern as follows:
1st row K1[p1, k1] to end.
Repeat this row until you have worked a square. Cast off.

Making these two swatches will help you understand how the continuity of the pattern is kept and you will then find it easier to see how to keep that continuity when you are shaping the shoe.

moss stitch shoes

sizes

To fit ages	3–6	9–12	12–18	months

materials

One 50g ball Debbie Bliss wool/cotton in Lilac.
Pair of 2¾mm (US 2) knitting needles.

tension

28 sts and 46 rows to 10cm/4in square over moss st on 2¾mm (US 2) needles.

abbreviations

alt = alternate **dec** = decrease **foll** = following **in** = inch(es) **inc** = increase one st by working into front and back of st **K(k)** = knit **mm** = millimetres **P(p)** = purl **rem** = remain **st(s)** = stitch(es) **tog** = together

moss stitch

1st row [K1, p1] to end.
2nd row [P1, k1] to end.
These 2 rows form moss st on an even number of sts.

to make

With 2¾mm (US 2) needles, cast on 22(26:30) sts.
Moss st 1 row.
Work in moss st and inc one st at each end of next and every foll alt row until there are 32(38:44) sts, work all increase sts in moss st, so keeping the continuity of the pattern.
Dec one st at each end of next and every foll alt row until 22(26:30) sts rem.
Shape heel
Next row Cast on 5(6:7) sts by cable method, moss st these 5(6:7) sts, then moss st to end. 27(32:37) sts.
Moss st 1 row.
Inc one st at end of next row and 4(5:6) foll alt rows. 32(38:44) sts.
Moss st 1 row.
Next row Cast off 20(22:24) sts, moss st to last st, inc in last st. 13(17:21) sts.
Moss st 10(14:18) rows.
Next row Work 2tog, moss st to end.
Next row Cast on 20(22:24) sts by cable method, moss st these 20(22:24) sts, then moss st to end. 32(38:44) sts.
Dec one st at beg of next and 4(5:6) foll alt rows. 27(32:37) sts.
Moss st 1 row.
Cast off.

to make up

Join back heel seam. Join upper to sole all around, easing in fullness at toes. Turn through to right side.

sweater with square set-in sleeves

All the garments so far have had a dropped shoulder, which is a shoulder line that comes down over the top of the arms because there is no shaping at the armhole. On baby designs there is no real need to have complicated arm or sleeve shaping but a good alternative to the dropped shoulder is the square set-in sleeve where stitches are cast off on the body and then the top of the sleeve slotted in and sewn to those cast-off stitches. It is a really simple shape but sometimes the instructions can be confusing to new, or even to more experienced knitters who have not tried them before. Because of this, I have shown the garment with the side and sleeve seams sewn up and before the sleeve has been sewn in (see detailed photograph on page 106). The stitch pattern used is a simple but pretty diamond pattern that shows up well in cotton.

sweater with square set-in sleeves

measurements						
To fit ages	3–6	6–9	12–18	24–36	months
Actual measurements					
Chest	54	60	66	72	cm
	21¼	23½	26	28¼	in
Length to shoulder	26	28	32	36	cm
	10¼	11	12½	14¼	in
Sleeve length	15	17	19	22	cm
	6	6¾	7½	8¾	in

materials

5(5:6:7) 50g balls of Debbie Bliss cotton double knitting in Ecru.
Pair each of 3¾mm (US 5) and 4mm (US 6) knitting needles.

tension

20 sts and 28 rows to 10cm/4in square over patt using 4mm (US 6) needles.

abbreviations

beg = beginning **cm** = centimetre(s) **cont** = continue **dec** = decrease **in** = inch(es)
inc = increase **K(k)** = knit **m1** = make one st by picking up the loop lying between the
st just worked and the next st and working into the back of it **mm** = millimetres
P(p) = purl **patt** = pattern **rem** = remaining **rep** = repeat **st(s)** = stitch(es)

back

With 3¾mm (US 5) needles, cast on 55(61:67:73) sts.
1st row (right side) K1, * p1, k1; rep from * to end.
2nd row P1, * k1, p1; rep from * to end.
Rep the last 2 rows 4(5:5:6) times more.
Change to 4mm (US 6) needles and work in pattern as follows:
1st row K3, * p1, k5; rep from * to last 4 sts, p1, k3.
2nd row P2, * k1, p1, k1, p3; rep from * to last 5 sts, k1, p1, k1, p2.
3rd row K1, * p1, k3, p1, k1; rep from * to end.
4th row K1, * p5, k1; rep from * to end.
5th row K1, * p1, k3, p1, k1; rep from * to end.
6th row P2, * k1, p1, k1, p3; rep from * to last 5 sts, k1, p1, k1, p2.
These 6 rows form the patt and are repeated throughout.
Cont in patt until work measures 16(17:19:21)cm/6¼(6¾:7½:8¼)in from cast-on edge, ending with a wrong side row.
Shape armholes
Cast off 6 sts at beg of next 2 rows. 43(49:55:61) sts.
Cont in patt until work measures 23(25:28:32)cm/9(10:11:12½)in from cast-on edge, ending with a wrong side row.
Shape neck
Next row Patt 14(16:19:21) sts, turn and work on these sts only for first side of neck.
Keeping continuity of pattern, dec one st at neck edge on next 4(4:6:6) rows.
10(12:13:15) sts.
Work 3 rows straight.
Shape shoulder
Cast off.
With right side facing, slip centre 15(17:17:19) sts onto a stitch holder, join on yarn to rem sts, patt to end.
Complete to match first side of neck, reversing all shapings.

front

Work exactly as given for back.

sleeves

With 3¾mm (US 5) needles, cast on 29(33:37:41) sts.
Work 9(9:11:13) rows rib as given for back.
Inc row (wrong side) Rib 2, m1, [rib 2, m1] 13(15:17:19) times, rib 1. 43(49:55:61) sts.
Work straight in patt as given for back until sleeve measures 15(17:19:22)cm/6(6¾:7½:8¾)in from cast-on edge, ending with a wrong side row.
Mark each end of last row with a coloured thread.
Work a further 6 rows.
Cast off.

neckband

Join right shoulder seam.
With right side facing, 3¾mm (US 5) needles, pick up and k10(10:11:11) sts down left side of front neck, k across 15(17:17:19) sts from front neck holder, pick up and k10(10:11:11) sts up right side of front neck, 9(9:10:10) sts down right back neck, k across 15(17:17:19) sts from back neck holder, pick up and k10(10:11:11) sts up left back neck. 69(73:77:81) sts.
Work 7(7:9:9) rows in rib as given for back.
Cast off in rib.

to make up

Join left shoulder and neckband seam. Sew sleeves into armholes, sewing the ends of the last 6 rows at top of sleeves above coloured thread markers to sts, cast off at under arm. Join side and sleeve seams.

raglan cardigan with fully fashioned shaping

Fully fashioned shaping is a term often used when types of increasing or decreasing are used to create a decorative effect and become a feature of the design. Usually the shaping is made a few stitches in from the edge so that it is clearly seen on the fabric rather than hidden in the seam, and can sometimes make sewing up or picking up stitches easier.

I have used such shaping on this raglan cardigan to emphasise the raglan sleeve, which can look really attractive on small, baby-sized garments and add style to a classic shape. Furthermore, with this shaping you can create a small decorative eyelet by not knitting into the back of the stitches when working the 'make ones' on the sleeve.

technique focus
decreasing (see also page 41)

slip 1, knit 1, pass slipped stitch over ('skpo')

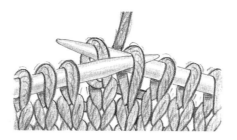

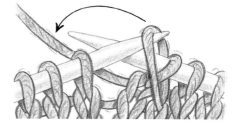

1 Insert the right-hand needle into the next stitch on the left-hand needle and slip it onto the right-hand needle without knitting it. Knit the next stitch. Then insert the left-hand needle into the slipped stitch as shown.

2 With the left-hand needle, lift the slipped stitch over the knitted stitch as shown and off the right-hand needle. One stitch has been decreased.

raglan cardigan with fully fashioned shaping

measurements	To fit ages	3–6	6–9	9–12	12–18 months
	Actual measurements				
	Chest	49	53	57	61	cm
		19¼	20¾	22½	24	in
	Length to shoulder	22	24	26	28	cm
		8¾	9½	10¼	11	in
	Sleeve length	14	16	18	20	cm
		5½	6¼	7	8	in

materials

4(5:5:6) 50g balls of Debbie Bliss cotton double knitting in Pale Blue.
Pair each of 3¼mm (US 3) and 4mm (US 6) needles.
5 buttons.

tension

20 sts and 28 rows to 10cm/4in square over st st using 4mm (US 6) needles.

abbreviations

beg = beginning **cm** = centimetre(s) **cont** = continue **foll** = following **in** = inch(es)
inc = increase **K(k)** = knit **m1** = make one st by picking up the loop lying between the
st just worked and the next st and working into the front of it **mm** = millimetres
P(p) = purl **rem** = remaining **rep** = repeat **skpo** = slip 1, k1, pass slipped st over
st(s) = stitch(es) **st st** = stocking stitch **tog** = together **yf** = yarn forward

back

With 3¼mm (US 3) needles, cast on 50(54:58:62) sts.

1st and 3rd sizes only

1st row P2, * k2, p2; rep from * to end.

2nd row K2, * p2, k2; rep from * to end.

2nd and 4th sizes only

1st row K2, * p2, k2; rep from * to end.

2nd row P2, * k2, p2; rep from * to end.

All sizes

Rep the last 2 rows 4 times more.

Change to 4mm (US 6) needles.

Beg with a k row, work in st st until back measures 11(12:13:14)cm/4¼(4¾:5:5½)in from cast-on edge, ending with a p row.

Shape raglan armhole

Cast off 3 sts at beg of next 2 rows.

1st row K2, skpo, k to last 4 sts, k2tog, k2.

2nd row P to end.

Rep the last 2 rows until 18(20:22:24) sts rem, ending with a k row.

Next row P2tog, p to last 2 sts, p2tog.

Leave these 16(18:20:22) sts on a stitch holder.

left front

With 3¼mm (US 3) needles, cast on 25(27:29:31) sts.

1st and 3rd sizes only

1st row P2, * k2, p2; rep from * to last 3 sts, k3.

2nd row P3, k2, * p2, k2; rep from * to end.

2nd and 4th sizes only

1st row K2, * p2, k2; rep from * to last 5 sts, p2, k3.

2nd row P3, * k2, p2; rep from * to end.

All sizes

Rep the last 2 rows 4 times more.

Change to 4mm (US 6) needles.

Beg with a k row, work in st st until front measures 11(12:13:14)cm/4¼(4¾:5:5½)in from cast-on edge, ending with a p row.

Shape raglan armhole

Next row Cast off 3 sts, k to end.

P 1 row.

1st row K2, skpo, k to end.
2nd row P to end.
Rep the last 2 rows until 9(10:11:12) sts rem, ending with a k row.
Next row P to last 2 sts, p2tog.
Leave these 8(9:10:11) sts on a holder.

right front

With 3¼mm (US 3) needles, cast on 25(27:29:31) sts.
1st and 3rd sizes only
1st row K3, p2, * k2, p2; rep from * to end.
2nd row K2, * p2, k2; rep from * to last 3 sts, p3.
2nd and 4th sizes only
1st row K3, * p2, k2; rep from * to end.
2nd row P2, * k2, p2; rep from * to last 5 sts, k2, p3.
All sizes
Rep the last 2 rows 4 times more.
Change to 4mm (US 6) needles.
Beg with a k row, work in st st until front measures 11(12:13:14)cm/4¼(4¾:5:5½)in from cast-on edge, ending with a k row.
Shape raglan armhole
Next row Cast off 3 sts, p to end.
1st row K to last 4 sts, k2 tog, k2.
2nd row P to end.
Rep the last 2 rows until 9(10:11:12) sts rem, ending with a k row.
Next row P2tog, p to end.
Leave these 8(9:10:11) sts on a stitch holder.

sleeves

With 3¼mm (US 3) needles, cast on 30(30:34:34) sts.
Work 10 rows in rib as given for 2nd and 4th sizes of back.
Change to 4mm (US 6) needles.
Beg with a k row, work in st st.
Work 2 rows.
Inc row (right side) K3, m1, k to last 3 sts, m1, k3.
Beg with a p row, work 3 rows in st st.
Cont in st st and inc one st as before at each end of the next row and every foll 4th row until there are 44(46:52:54) sts.

Cont straight until sleeve measures 14(16:18:20)cm/5½(6¼:7:8)in from cast-on edge, ending with a p row.

Shape raglan top
Cast off 3 sts at beg of next 2 rows.
1st row K2, skpo, k to last 4 sts, k2tog, k2.
2nd row P to end.
Rep the last 2 rows until 12(12:16:16) sts rem, ending with a k row.
Next row P2tog, p to last 2 sts, p2tog.
Leave these 10(10:14:14) sts on a stitch holder.

neckband

Join raglan seams.
With right side facing and 3¼mm (US 3) needles, k8(9:10:11) sts from right front, k10(10:14:14) sts from right sleeve, k16(18:20:22) sts from back, k10(10:14:14) sts from left sleeve, then k8(9:10:11) sts from left front. 52(56:68:72) sts.
1st row (wrong side) P3, * k2, p2; rep from * to last 5 sts, k2, p3.
2nd row K3, * p2, k2; rep from * to last 5 sts, p2, k3.
Rep the 1st and 2nd rows once more and the 1st row again.
Cast off in rib.

button band

With right side facing and 3¼mm (US 3) needles, pick up and k50(54:58:62) sts along left front edge.
Beg with a 2nd row, work 5 rows in rib as given for 2nd and 4th sizes of back.
Cast off in rib.

buttonhole band

With right side facing and 3¼mm (US 3) needles, pick up and k50(54:58:62) sts along right front edge.
Beg with a 2nd row, work 2 rows in rib as given for 2nd and 4th sizes of back.
Buttonhole row (wrong side) Rib 2, [rib 2tog, yf, rib 9(10:11:12) sts] 4 times, rib 2tog, yf, rib 2.
Rib 2 rows.
Cast off in rib.

to make up

Join side and sleeve seams. Sew on buttons.

dress with eyelets

By using the eyelet buttonhole used in the moss stitch cushion project (see page 79) you can create a decorative lace detail that is perfect for baby knits. Simply by bringing the yarn forward and then decreasing afterwards, you make holes that are ideal for threading through ribbon or cord.

This sleeveless dress has a small back opening to make sure that the neck will go over the baby's head but also fit snugly when it is on. To get over the problem of pulling neck openings over struggling babies, designers will quite often use a shoulder fastening as an alternative to a back neck opening.

dress with eyelets

measurements	To fit ages	3–6	9–12	12–18	18–24 months
	Actual measurements				
	Chest	47	52	56	61	cm
		18½	20½	22	24	in
	Length to shoulder	36	41	49	55	cm
		14¼	16	19¼	21¾	in

materials

4(5:6:7) 50g balls Debbie Bliss wool/cotton in Ecru.
Pair each of 2¾mm (US 2) and 3¼mm (US 3) needles.
2¾mm (US 2) circular needle.
1 button.
Approximately 122cm/48in narrow ribbon.

tension

25 sts and 34 rows to 10cm/4in square over st st using 3¼mm (US 3) needles.

abbreviations

alt = alternate **beg** = beginning **cm** = centimetre(s) **cont** = continue **dec** = decrease
foll = following **in(s)** = inch(es) **K(k)** = knit **P(p)** = purl **rem** = remaining **rep** = repeat
skpo = slip 1 st, k1, pass slipped st over **st(s)** = stitch(es) **st st** = stocking stitch
tog = together **yf** = yarn forward

back

** With 3¼mm (US 3) needles, cast on 101(109:117:125) sts.
K 5 rows.
Beg with a k row, work 6 rows in st st.
Dec row (right side) K10(11:12:13), skpo, k to last 12(13:14:15) sts, k2tog,
k10(11:12:13).
Work 5(7:9:11) rows in st st.
Rep the last 6(8:10:12) rows until 81(89:97:105) sts rem.
Cont straight until back measures 23(27:34:39)cm/9(10½:13½:15¼)in from cast-on edge,
ending with a p row.
Dec row K1, [k2tog, yf, skpo] 20(22:24:26) times. 61(67:73:79) sts.
Cont straight until back measures 26(30:37:42)cm/10¼(11¾:14½:16½)in from cast-on
edge, ending with a p row.
Shape armholes
Cast off 6 sts at beg of next 2 rows and 4 sts at beg of foll 2 rows.
Dec one st at each end of the next and every foll alt row until 31(37:43:49) sts rem.

P 1 row. **
Back opening
Next row K14(17:20:23) sts, turn and work on these sts for first side of back opening.
Next row Cast on 3 sts, k these 3 sts, then p to end.
Next row K to end.
Next row K3, p to end.
Rep the last 2 rows until back measures 33(38:46:52)cm/13(15:18:20½)in from cast-on edge, ending with a wrong side row.
Shape neck
Next row K to last 6(8:8:10) sts, leave these sts on a stitch holder, turn.
Dec one st at neck edge on every row until 5(7:9:11) sts rem.
Cont straight until back measures 36(41:49:55)cm/14¼(16:19¼:21¾)in from cast-on edge, ending with a p row.
Shape shoulder
Cast off.
With right side facing, rejoin yarn to rem sts, k to end.
Next row P to last 3 sts, k3.
Next row K to end.
Repeat the last 2 rows until back measures 33(38:46:52)cm/13(15:18:20½)in from cast-on edge, ending with a wrong side row.
Shape neck
Next row K6(8:8:10) sts, leave these sts on a holder, k to end.
Dec one st at neck edge on every row until 5(7:9:11) sts rem.
Cont straight until back measures 36(41:49:55)cm/14¼(16:19¼:21¾)in from cast-on edge, ending with a p row.
Shape shoulder
Cast off.

front

Work as given for back from ** to **.
Shape neck
Next row (right side) K11(13:15:17) sts, turn and work on these sts for first side of neck shaping.
Dec 1 st at neck edge on every foll alt row until 5(7:9:11) sts rem.
Cont without further shaping until front measures same as back to shoulder, ending at side edge.
Shape shoulder
Cast off.
With right side facing, slip centre 9(11:13:15) sts onto a stitch holder, rejoin yarn to rem sts, k to end.
Complete to match first side, reversing shaping.

neckband

Join shoulder seams.
With right side facing and 2¾mm (US 2) circular knitting needle, slip 6(8:8:10) sts from left back onto needle, pick up and k9 sts up left back to shoulder, 17(17:18:19) sts down left front neck, k across 9(11:13:15) sts from front neck holder, pick up and k17(17:18:19) sts up right front neck to shoulder, 9 sts from right back neck, k across 6(8:8:10) sts on back neck holder. 73(79:83:91) sts.
Work backwards and forwards in rows.
K 1 row.
Buttonhole row K1, yf, k2tog, k to end.
K 1 row.
Cast off.

armbands

Join left shoulder and neckband seam.
With right side facing and 2¾mm (US 2) knitting needles, pick up and k60(66:72:78) sts evenly around armhole edge.
K 3 rows.
Cast off.

to make up

Join side and armband seams.
Lap buttonband behind buttonhole band and catch cast-on sts in place. Sew on button.
Thread ribbon through eyelets to tie at centre front.

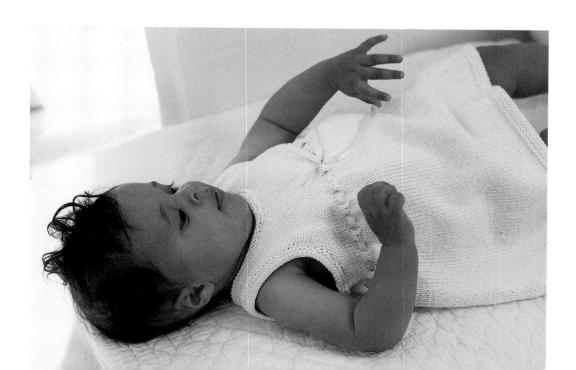

shawl-collared jacket

This boxy jacket has one of my favourite details, a cosy shawl collar. Collars are usually easy to knit but it is important that they fit properly around the neck, particularly on babies' rather short ones! One of the essentials of a well-fitting collar is to make sure there is ease in the back neck, and one of the best ways of achieving this is to use turning rows.

Turning rows, or short rows as they are also called, are used to shape the outside edge of your work without having to increase or decrease. Instead of working to the end of the row, you knit part of the row, turn the work, and work back, creating a shorter row. By doing this you are working the stitches in part of the row more than other stitches. In this way you can make darts, slope shoulders or turn the heel of socks. By using it on the collar at the back of the neck, you create a bias effect that provides the ease needed at the back neck. When you turn the work before completing the row, you can make a small hole. Sometimes, slipping a stitch, as in the construction of the shawl-collared jacket, can prevent this.

However, on stocking stitch in particular, the gap between the rows can be more marked, and 'wrapping' the stitch can make a smoother transition between the two levels of knitting.

wrapping yarn

1 Knit the number of stitches needed for the short row, bring the yarn forward between the stitches, slip the next stitch purlwise, then take the yarn back.

2 Return the slipped stitch to the left needle, ready to turn and work the next short row.

You may like the look of the wrap around the stitch and use it as a decorative detail. If not, get rid of it on the next long row by working it together with the wrapped stitch thus. Knit to the first stitch that has a loop or wrap made around it, slip this stitch from the left-hand needle to the right-hand needle at the same time lifting the wrap up onto the right-hand needle, making an extra stitch. Place the two stitches back on to the left-hand needle and knit them together.

shawl-collared jacket

measurements	To fit ages	6–12	12–18	18–24	months
	Actual measurements				
	Chest	62	70	80	cm
		24½	27½	31½	in
	Length to shoulder	30	33	36	cm
		11¾	13	14¼	in
	Sleeve seam	16	18	23	cm
		6¼	7	9	in

materials

4(5:5) 50g balls Debbie Bliss merino aran in Stone.
Pair of 5mm (US 8) knitting needles.
4 buttons.

tension

18 sts and 24 rows to 10cm/4in square over st st using 5mm (US 8) needles.

abbreviations

alt = alternate **beg** = beginning **cm** = centimetre(s) **cont** = continue **foll** = following **in(s)** = inch(es) **inc** = increase **K(k)** = knit **m1** = make one st by picking up the loop lying between the st just worked and the next st and working into the back of it **P(p)** = purl **rem** = remaining **rep** = repeat **sl** = slip **st(s)** = stitch(es) **st st** = stocking stitch **tbl** = through back loop **tog** = together **yo** = yarn over needle

back

With 5mm (US 8) needles, cast on 54(62:70) sts.
1st row (right side) K2, * p2, k2; rep from * to end.
2nd row P2, * k2, p2; rep from * to end.
Rep these 2 rows 1(2:2) time(s) more.
Next row (right side) K13, m1, k28(36:44), m1, k13. 56(64:72) sts.
Beg with a p row, work in st st until back measures 30(33:36)cm/11¾(13:14¼)in from cast-on edge, ending with a p row.
Shape shoulders
Cast off 7(9:11) sts at beg of next 2 rows, then 8(9:10) sts at beg of foll 2 rows.
Leave rem 26(28:30) sts on a stitch holder for collar.

left front

With 5mm (US 8) needles, cast on 27(31:35) sts.
1st row (right side) K2, * p2, k2; rep from * to last st, k1.
2nd row P3, * k2, p2; rep from * to end.
Rep these 2 rows 1(2:2) time(s) more.

Beg with a k row, work in st st until front measures 19(21:23)cm/7½(8¼:9)in from cast-on edge, ending with a p row.

Shape neck

Next row (right side) K to last 3 sts, k2tog, k1.

P 1 row.

Rep the last 2 rows 11(12:13) times more. 15(18:21) sts.

Work straight until front measures same as back to shoulder, ending with a p row.

Shape shoulder

Cast off 7(9:11) sts at beg of next row.

P 1 row.

Cast off rem 8(9:10) sts.

right front

With 5mm (US 8) needles, cast on 27(31:35) sts.

1st row (right side) K3, * p2, k2; rep from * to end.

2nd row P2, * k2, p2; rep from * to last st, p1.

Rep these 2 rows 1(2:2) times more.

Beg with a k row, work in st st until front measures 19(21:23)cm/7½(8¼:9)in from cast-on edge, ending with a p row.

Shape neck

Next row (right side) K1, k2tog tbl, k to end.

P 1 row.

Rep the last 2 rows 11(12:13) times more. 15(18:21) sts.

Work straight until front measures same as back to shoulder, ending with a k row.

Shape shoulder

Cast off 7(9:11) sts at beg of next row.

K 1 row.

Cast off rem 8(9:10) sts.

sleeves

With 5mm (US 8) needles, cast on 26(30:34) sts.

1st row (right side) K2, * p2, k2; rep from * to end.

2nd row P2, * k2, p2; rep from * to end.

Rep these 2 rows 2(3:3) times more.

Next row (right side) K4(3:5), [m1, k6(8:8)] 3 times, m1, k4(3:5). 30(34:38) sts.

Beg with a p row, work in st st and inc one st as before at each end of every foll 4th row, until there are 44(50:56) sts.

Work straight until sleeve measures 16(18:23)cm/6¼(7:9)in from cast-on edge, ending with a p row.

Cast off.

collar and front bands

Join shoulder seams.

With right side facing and 5mm (US 8) needles, pick up and k44(46:48) sts up right front edge to beg of neck shaping, 30(31:32) sts up right front neck to shoulder, k across 26(28:30) sts from centre back neck holder, pick up and k30(31:32) sts down left front neck to beg of neck shaping and 44(46:48) sts down left front to cast-on edge. 174(182:190) sts.

Beg with a 2nd row, work 1 row in rib as given for back.

1st row (right side) Rib 92(98:104) sts, turn.

2nd row Sl 1, rib 9(13:17), turn.

3rd row Sl 1, rib 13(17:21), turn.

4th row Sl 1, rib 17(21:25), turn.

5th row Sl 1, rib 21(25:29), turn.

6th row Sl 1, rib 25(29:33), turn.

Cont to work a further 14 turning rows in this way, working an extra 4 sts, as before, on each row.

Next row Rib to end.

Buttonhole row (wrong side) Rib 134(139:144) sts, [yo, work 2tog, rib 10(11:12)] 3 times, yo, work 2tog, rib 2.

Rib 1 row.

Cast off in rib.

to make up

Matching centre of cast-off edge of sleeve to shoulder seam, sew on sleeves. Join side and sleeve seams. Sew on buttons to match buttonholes.

two-needle socks

Socks are never particularly easy to make if you have never tackled them before but the results are so charming that I think they are well worth the effort. For the perfect socks they should really be knitted on four needles to prevent a seam. But four small needles can be a nightmare to use on such tiny pieces so I have chosen a yarn containing cashmere to make even the seam as soft as possible.

The yarn obviously needs to be a fine one for the finished sock but as this will be your first attempt at shaping heels and insteps, I really do advise you to work a practice piece in a thicker yarn on bigger needles first. In this way you can see your shapings for the heel and clearly observe the row ends when you come to pick up stitches for the instep. So relax; the pattern works but you are in unfamiliar territory. When you see how your practice piece works, you can tackle the real thing with confidence.

two-needle socks

sizes	**To fit ages**		3	6	months

materials
One 50g ball Debbie Bliss baby cashmerino in Pale Blue.
Pair of 3¼mm (US 3) knitting needles.

tension
25 sts and 34 rows to 10cm/4in square over st st using 3¼mm (US 3) needles.

abbreviations
beg = beginning **cm** = centimetre(s) **dec** = decrease **in** = inch(es) **K(k)** = knit
mm = millimetres **P(p)** = purl **rem** = remaining **skpo** = slip 1, knit 1, pass slipped stitch
over **sl** = slip **st(s)** = stitch(es) **st st** = stocking stitch **tbl** = through back loop
tog = together

to make (make 2)
With 3¼mm (US 3) needles, cast on 36(40) sts.
Rib row * K1, p1; rep from * to end.
Rib a further 5(7) rows.
Beg with a k row, work in st st.
Work 2(4) rows.
Dec row K5, k2tog, k to last 7 sts, skpo, k5.
Work 5(7) rows.
Dec row K4, k2tog, k to last 6 sts, skpo, k4.
Work 3(5) rows.
Dec row K3, [k2tog, k6(7)] 3 times, k2tog, k3(4). 28(32) sts.
Shape heel
Next row P8(9) sts only, turn.
Work 9 rows in st st on these 8(9) sts only.
Dec row P2(3), p2tog, p1, turn.
Next row Sl 1, k3(4).
Dec row P3(4), p2tog, p1, turn.
Next row Sl 1, k4(5).
Dec row P4(5), p2tog.
Break yarn and leave rem 5(6) sts on a stitch holder.
With wrong side facing, slip centre 12(14) sts onto a stitch holder, rejoin yarn to rem 8(9) sts, p to end.
Work 8 rows in st st on these 8(9) sts.
Dec row K2(3), skpo, k1, turn.

Next row Sl 1, p3(4).
Dec row K3(4), skpo, k1, turn.
Next row Sl 1, p4(5).
Dec row K4(5), skpo, turn.
Next row Sl 1, p4(5).
Shape instep
Next row K5(6), pick up and k8 sts evenly along inside edge of heel, k12(14) sts from holder, pick up and k8 sts along inside edge of heel and k5(6) sts from holder. 38(42) sts.
P 1 row.
Dec row K11(12), k2tog, k12(14), skpo, k11(12).
P 1 row.
Dec row K10(11), k2tog, k12(14), skpo, k10(11).
P 1 row.
Dec row K9(10), k2tog, k12(14), skpo, k9(10).
P 1 row.
Dec row K8(9), k2 tog, k12(14), skpo, k8(9). 30(34) sts.
Work 13(17) rows straight.
Shape toe
Dec row K1, [skpo, k5(6)] 4 times, k1.
P 1 row.
Dec row K1, [skpo, k4(5)] 4 times, k1.
P 1 row.
Dec row K1, [skpo, k3(4)] 4 times, k1.
P 1 row.
Dec row K1, [skpo, k2(3)] 4 times, k1.
2nd size only
P 1 row.
Dec row K1, [skpo, k(2)] 4 times, k1.
Both sizes
Dec row [P2tog] 7 times.
Break yarn, thread through rem sts, pull up and secure. Join seam.

scarf with pocket

Simply by sewing a seam you can turn this scarf into a hooded woolly warmer, perfect for snuggling into, with the scarf ties making it practical too. I have added a pocket for decorative detail – and because I know children always lose their gloves.

Working pockets into the main piece of the garment always gives a much neater finish than stitching on patch pockets afterwards. Sometimes the instructions can appear confusing but the basic idea is quite simple. The pocket lining, which will form the back of the pocket, is worked first and knitted to the size and length required. The stitches are not cast off but left on a stitch holder or spare needle.

When the main piece is knitted to the point at which the pocket opening will be, the stitches of that row are worked to the position of the pocket and the same number of stitches as the pocket lining are cast off. On the next row, at the position where the stitches were cast off, rather than casting on stitches you work across the stitches on the holder, and then carry on to the end of the row. The pocket lining has now become integrated into the main body, with an opening at the front.

If you want a border on the top of the pocket, leave the stitches on a stitch holder and then work a stitch pattern such as a rib on those stitches later. The pocket lining is sewn to the back of the garment. To keep the linings square when stitching them in place, tack colour guidelines in a contrast thread on the right side of the work.

scarf with pocket

size	**To fit ages** 1–2 years
materials	Four 50g balls of Debbie Bliss cashmerino aran in Teal (M). One 50g ball in Ecru (C). Pair of 5mm (US 8) needles.
tension	33 sts and 25 rows to 10cm/4in square over unstretched rib pattern using 5mm (US 8) needles.
abbreviations	**cm** = centimetre(s) **cont** = continue **in** = inch(es) **K(k)** = knit **mm** = millimetres **P(p)** = purl **rep** = repeat **st(s)** = stitch(es).
pocket lining	With 5mm (US 8) needles and C, cast on 38 sts. **1st row** (right side) P2, * k2, p2; rep from * to end. **2nd row** K2, * p2, k2; rep from * to end. Rep the last 2 rows 12 times more and the 1st row again. Leave sts on a stitch holder.
scarf	With 5mm (US 8) needles and M, cast on 50 sts. **1st row** (right side) K2, * p2, k2; rep from * to end. **2nd row** P2, * k2, p2; rep from * to end. Rep the last 2 rows 12 times more. **Place pocket** **Next row** (right side) Rib 6, cast off next 38 sts in rib, rib to end. **Next row** Rib 6, rib across sts of pocket lining, rib to end. Cont in rib until scarf measures 126cm/49½in from cast-on edge, ending with a wrong side row. Cast off in rib.
to make up	Sew pocket lining to wrong side of scarf. Fold scarf in two, so that cast-off edge is level with top of pocket. Join the back seam for 15cm/6in down from the fold to form the hood. Gently press the scarf but only where it forms the hood.

v-neck sweater with pockets

Here is a classic V-neck sweater with a dash of colour on the ribs in which you can use most of the techniques you have learnt so far. There are increasings on the sleeve, decreasings and picking up stitches along the neckline and pockets with picked up ribbed borders. Sewing up and darning in ends completes the garment. Complete this sweater and you can now consider yourself an accomplished knitter.

v-neck sweater with pockets

measurements					
	To fit ages	3–6	6–9	12–18	months
	Actual measurements				
	Chest	51	57	64	cm
		20	22½	25½	in
	Length to shoulder	26	28	32	cm
		10¼	11	12½	in
	Sleeve length	16	19	22	cm
		6¼	7½	8¾	in

materials

3(4:4) 50g balls of Debbie Bliss baby cashmerino in Ecru (M).
One 50g ball in Pale Blue (C).
Pair each of 3mm (US 2) and 3¼mm (US 3) knitting needles.

tension

25 sts and 34 rows to 10cm/4in square over st st using 3¼mm (US 3) needles.

abbreviations

alt = alternate **beg** = beginning **cm** = centimetre(s) **cont** = continue **foll** = following **in(s)** = inch(es) **inc** = increase **K(k)** = knit **m1** = make one st by picking up the loop lying between the st just worked and the next st and working into the back of it **P(p)** = purl **rem** = remaining **rep** = repeat **skpo** = slip 1, knit 1, pass slipped st over **st(s)** = stitch(es) **st st** = stocking stitch **tog** = together

back

With 3mm (US 2) needles and C, cast on 66(74:82) sts.
1st rib row K2, * p2, k2; rep from * to end.
2nd rib row P2, * k2, p2; rep from * to end.
Change to M.
Rep the last 2 rows twice more.
Change to 3¼mm (US 3) needles.
Beg with a k row, work in st st until back measures 15(16:18)cm/6(6¼:7)in from cast-on edge, ending with a p row.
Shape armholes
Cast off 3 sts at beg of next 2 rows.
Next row K2, skpo, k to last 2 sts, k2tog, k2.
Next row P to end.
Rep the last 2 rows 2(3:4) times. 54(60:66) sts.
Cont in st st until back measures 26(28:32)cm/10¼(11:12½)in from cast-on edge, ending with a p row.
Shape shoulders
Cast off 13(14:15) sts at beg of next 2 rows.
Leave rem 28(32:36) sts on a stitch holder.

pocket linings (make 2)

With 3¼mm (US 3) needles and M, cast on 18(22:22) sts.
Beg with a k row, work 22(28:28) rows in st st.
Leave these sts on a stitch holder.

front

With 3mm (US 2) needles and C, cast on 66(74:82) sts.
1st rib row K2, * p2, k2; rep from * to end.
2nd rib row P2, * k2, p2; rep from * to end.
Change to M.
Rep the last 2 rows twice more.
Change to 3¼mm (US 3) needles.
Beg with a k row, work 22(28:28) rows in st st.
Place pockets
Next row K8(8:12), place next 18(22:22) sts on a stitch holder, k across 18(22:22) sts of 1st pocket lining, k14, place next 18(22:22) sts on a stitch holder, k across 18(22:22) sts of 2nd pocket lining, k8(8:12).
Cont in st st until back measures 15(16:18)cm/6(6¼:7)in from cast-on edge, ending with a p row.
Shape armholes
Cast off 3 sts at beg of next 2 rows.
Next row K2, skpo, k to last 2 sts, k2tog, k2.
Next row P to end.

Rep the last 2 rows 2(3:4) times. 54(60:66) sts.
P 1 row.
Shape front neck
Next row K22(25:28) sts, k2tog, k2, turn and work on these sts for first side of front neck.
Next row P to end.
Next row K to last 4 sts, k2 tog, k2.
Rep the last 2 rows until 13(14:15) sts rem.
Cont straight until front measures same as back to shoulder, ending at armhole edge.
Shape shoulder
Cast off.
With right side facing, slip centre 2 sts onto a safety pin, join on yarn to rem sts.
Next row K2, skpo, k to end.
Next row P to end
Next row K2, skpo, k to last end.
Rep the last 2 rows until 13(14:15) sts rem.
Cont straight until front measures same as back to shoulder, ending at armhole edge.
Shape shoulder
Cast off.

sleeves

With 3mm (US 2) needles and C, cast on 38(38:42) sts.
1st rib row K2, * p2, k2; rep from * to end.
2nd rib row P2, * k2, p2; rep from * to end.
Change to M.
Rep the last 2 rows twice more.
Change to 3¼mm (US 3) needles.
Beg with a k row, work 2 rows in st st.
Next row K3, m1, k to last 3 sts, m1, k3.
Cont in st st and inc one st, as before, at each end of every foll 4th row until there are 60(66:74) sts.
Cont straight until sleeve measures 16(19:22)cm/6¼(7½:8¾)in from cast-on edge, ending with a p row.
Cast off 3 sts at beg of next 2 rows.
Dec one st at each end of the next and 2(3:4) foll alt rows. 48(52:58) sts.
Cast off.

neckband

Join right shoulder seam.
With right side facing, using 3mm (US 3) needles and M, pick up and k26(30:34) sts evenly down left side of front neck, k2 from safety pin, pick up and k26(30:34) sts evenly up right side of front neck, k28(32:36) sts from back neck holder. 82(94:106) sts.

1st row K2, * p2, k2; rep from * to end.
2nd row Rib 25(29:33), k2tog, skpo, rib to end.
3rd row Rib to end.
4th row Rib 24(28:32), k2tog, skpo, rib to end.
Cut off M, join on C.
5th row Rib to end.
6th row Rib 23(27:31), k2tog, skpo, rib to end.
Cast off in rib.

pocket tops

With right side facing, using 3mm (US 3) needles and M, work across sts for pocket tops
as follows:
Next row K2, * p2, k2; rep from * to end.
Next row P2, * k2, p2; rep from * to end.
Rep the last 2 rows once more.
Change to C.
Work 2 more rows in rib.
Cast off in rib.

to make up

Join right shoulder and neckband seam. Sew sleeves into armholes. Sew down pocket
linings and pocket tops. Join side and sleeve seams.

stockists

For stockists of Debbie Bliss Yarns please contact:

UK
Designer Yarns Ltd,
Units 8–10,
Newbridge Industrial Estate,
Pitt Street, Keighley,
W. Yorkshire, BD21 4PQ
Tel: +44 01535 664222
Fax: +44 01535 664333
e-mail:
lauren@designeryarns.uk.com

USA
Knitting Fever Inc.,
35 Debevoise Avenue,
Roosevelt, New York 11575
Tel: +01 516 546 3600
Fax: +01 516 546 6871
www.knittingfever.com

CANADA
Diamond Yarns Ltd,
155 Martin Ross Avenue,
Unit 3, Toronto, Ontario M3J 2L9.
Tel: +01 416 736 6111
Fax: +01 416 736 6112
www.diamondyarn.com

JAPAN
Eisaku Noro & Co. Ltd,
55 Shimoda Ohibino Azaichou,
Ichinomita Aichi, 491 0105
Tel: +81 52 203 5100
Fax: +81 52 203 5077

GERMANY
Designer Yarns,
Handelsagentur Klaus Koch,
Pontinusweg 7,
D-50859 Köln
Tel/Fax: +49 0234 77573
www.designer-yarns.de

FRANCE
Elle Tricote,
8 Rue de Cog,
67000 Strasbourg
Tel: +33 03 88 230313
Fax: +33 03 88 230169
www.elletricote.com.fr

BELGIUM
Pavan,
Koningin Astridlaan 78,
9000 Gent
Tel: +32 9221 8594
e-mail: pavan@pandora.be

AUSTRALIA
Jo Sharp Pty Ltd,
PO Box 1018,
Fremantle, WA 6959
Tel: +61 08 9430 9699
e-mail: yarn@josharp.com.au

index